Domus Dei Porta Coeli
House of God, Gate of Heaven

Every bishop, I feel certain, has a deep feeling of pride about his cathedral church, whether it be a humble chapel or a great vaulting edifice. My particular pride about St. James Cathedral comes not so much from its extraordinary beauty as from a realization of just how holy the place is—a holiness absorbed for nearly one-hundred years now from God's holy people who have gathered there to pray and to celebrate the Sacraments of our church. It is no wonder, then, that whenever I walk into St. James Cathedral, I find myself with Jacob of old, wanting to cry aloud those words captured in the floor mosaic at the cathedral's main entrance, *"How awesome is this place! This is none other than the* House of God and the Gate of Heaven!"

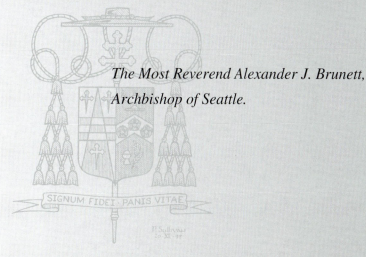

The Most Reverend Alexander J. Brunett,
Archbishop of Seattle.

House of GOD
Gate of Heaven

A view through the oculus *above the altar.*

Designed and edited by Jackie O'Ryan

Seattle's St. James CATHEDRAL

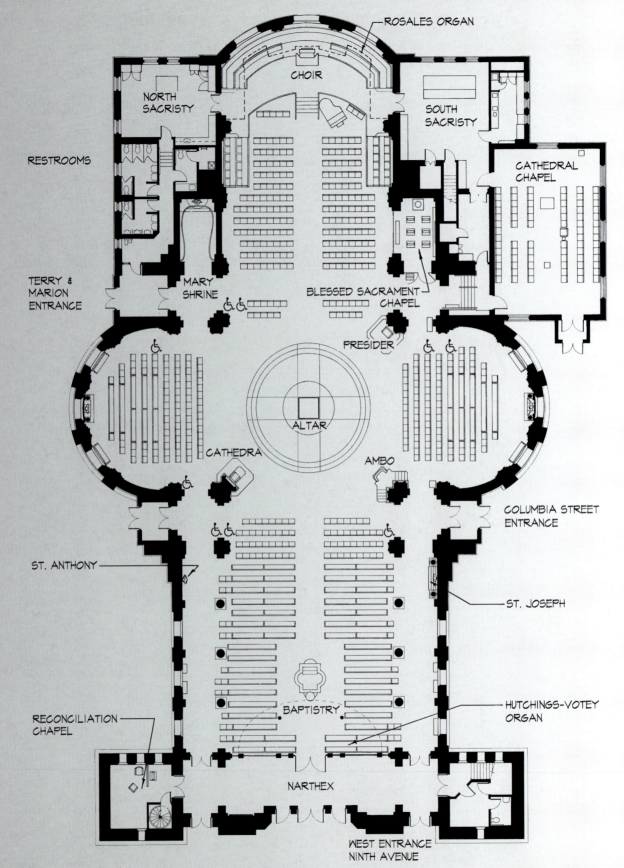

ROSALES ORGAN

CHOIR

NORTH
SACRISTY

SOUTH
SACRISTY

RESTROOMS

CATHEDRAL
CHAPEL

TERRY &
MARION
ENTRANCE

MARY
SHRINE

BLESSED SACRAMENT
CHAPEL

PRESIDER

ALTAR

CATHEDRA

COLUMBIA STREET
ENTRANCE

AMBO

ST. ANTHONY

ST. JOSEPH

RECONCILIATION
CHAPEL

BAPTISTRY

HUTCHINGS-VOTEY
ORGAN

NARTHEX

WEST ENTRANCE
NINTH AVENUE

St. James Cathedral Floor Plan

CONTENTS

Seattle's St. James Cathedral

FOREWORD
DOMUS DEI PORTA COELI

The Very Reverend Michael G. Ryan

For nearly a century, St. James Cathedral has stood high atop Seattle's First Hill. In 1904, when he arrived here from Vancouver, Washington, site of the first St. James Cathedral, Bishop Edward O'Dea put the people of Seattle on notice that the Catholic Church was here to stay. In building his cathedral church in a place where it couldn't be missed, and in entrusting its design to a prestigious New York architectural firm whose other project at the time was New York's great Cathedral of St. John the Divine, the bishop underscored his point. He also quietly validated the claim Seattle's first pioneers had made for their fledgling settlement that day in 1851 when they had beached their boats on a promontory west of Seattle and christened it, in the local language of the natives, "New York Alki" (New York by-and-by).

Was it whimsy or vision that prompted such an outlandish claim on the part of those intrepid settlers? Who can say? But this much is certain: whimsy was not part of the vocabulary of Edward John O'Dea.

In the cathedral's early years pioneers still walked Seattle's streets, and noisy cable cars clanged their way up and down its daunting hills. Awkwardly but rather grandly, the cathedral stood sentinel-like over a city that was still waking up.

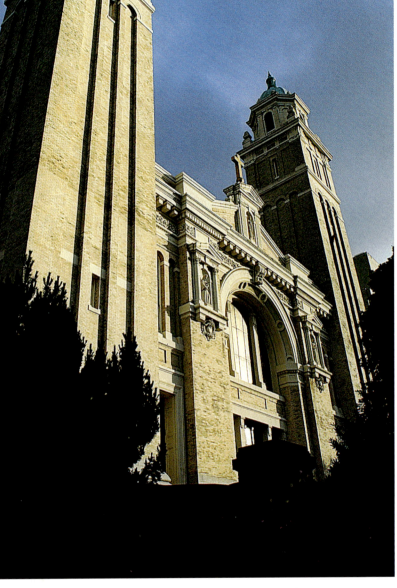

**St. James Cathedral plays both sentinel and beacon
as it stands watch over a vibrant city,
calling people to prayer, challenging them to justice,
enticing them with beauty.**

In those days, the cathedral *was* Seattle's skyline. No serious challenger appeared until 1914, when the Smith Tower brought yet another mention of Manhattan to a growing but still provincial city.

Domus Dei

Now, at the dawning of a new century and a new millennium, partially eclipsed by towering high-rises that stand taller and darker even than the giant firs and cedars that once crowned First Hill, St. James Cathedral plays both sentinel and beacon as it stands watch over a vibrant city, calling people to prayer, challenging them to justice, enticing them with beauty.

All humans value signs; Catholics value them more than most. Signs point to unseen realities and the most successful ones have power not only to point but to make present, thereby becoming Sacraments, meeting places with God. Cathedrals are such signs. They draw on the best humans have to offer, whether in art, architecture, or music, and they offer, in return, a glimpse of God, even a preview of heaven. It is surely no secret, then, that the first image to greet the person entering St. James Cathedral, high in the tympanum above the central bronze doors, is the heavenly city of the Book of Revelation, and that the first words to speak, in the mosaic just inside the front doors, are DOMUS DEI PORTA COELI ("House of God, Gate of Heaven").

But heaven does not stop at the front doors. The focal point of St. James Cathedral is its centrally placed altar, a gleaming white vision in stone of the heavenly banquet table. The entire geography of the cathedral – baptistry, ambo, *cathedra*, chapels, shrines, windows, processional paths and vaulted ceiling – makes sense only in relation to the altar, and the people who gather around the altar make sense of the building and bring it to life.

That is as it should be, because more important by far than any cathedral building are the people who go there. A cathedral fulfills its highest calling not by being the church but by becoming a house for God's people: *the church*. In solemn rituals as well as in quiet, whispered prayer, anonymous people become an awakened people and self-absorbed people become a servant people, thanks to the power of Christ radiating from the altar of sacrifice, the Christ who is *"in our midst as one who serves."*

Every cathedral has its own special genius. Perhaps the special genius of Seattle's St. James Cathedral is its power both to gather people in a unique way and to send them forth. Every day of the year the cathedral gathers to its heart an astonishingly diverse family of people *"from every race, nation, people and tongue."* Many, of course, find their way to the altar, where they feast on the Bread of Life; others feast on other life-giving breads: the bread of the Word, the bread of loving human service, the bread of artistic beauty. All find themselves sent forth from the cathedral changed in some way: nourished, challenged, uplifted.

The embrace of any cathedral should be wide. Sooner or later, people of all faiths and of no faith at all find their way there. St. James is no exception. From its earliest days right up to the present, St. James Cathedral has welcomed all people of good will who entered its doors. The future will be no different. St. James will continue to be not only a church but a crossroads and a center: a crossroads where people explore ideas old and new in light of the Gospel; a center for cultural and ecumenical events which help to shape the fabric of a vital urban community.

The pages which follow are meant to picture and portray some of the holy and beautiful people and things that make up St. James Cathedral. They will have served their purpose if they further awaken all who enter its doors to the surpassing beauty of this House of God, this Gate of Heaven made holy by God's abiding presence and by the prayers of countless people who, for nearly a century, have met the living God in St. James Cathedral. ❏

Father Michael G. Ryan,
pastor of St. James Cathedral

PORTA COELI
the Bronze Ceremonial Doors

The center ceremonial doors were opened for the first time on the eve of the Third Christian Millennium.

The bronze ceremonial doors of St. James Cathedral, completed and dedicated on the eve of the Third Christian Millennium, tell of the great procession of the human family toward the heavenly city and invite all who come to the cathedral to take their place in that great procession.

The doors are the work of the renowned German artist, Ulrich Henn, whose sculptures grace cathedrals and churches all over Germany, and whose bronze gates at National Cathedral in Washington, D.C., are among the treasures of that celebrated structure.

The procession depicted on the doors begins as Adam and Eve leave the delights of the Garden of Eden, with its Tree of Life laden with every desirable fruit. The angel sends them off on a long journey where

These three scenes are depictions from the Old Testament presented in deep bronze relief on the left central door.

loneliness, hard work, and even death will be the daily results of a growing alienation from God (Genesis 3). The journey leads through many dark days and eventually into the dark waters of the Great Flood. A reconciling moment comes when God enters a covenant with Noah and his family, setting a rainbow in the sky as an abiding sign of divine favor (Genesis 9). But the journey is far from over. Long years of exile and slavery in Egypt await God's people until that defining event of the entire Old Testament, when God raises up Moses to lead the chosen people from slavery to freedom through the waters of the Red Sea (Exodus 14).

The procession continues with the coming of Jesus, whose baptism in the Jordan (Mark 1), a new Exodus, starts him off on a journey of bringing "glad tidings to the poor, liberty to captives and recovery of sight to the blind

(Luke 4). The doors tell this story through three events from Jesus' ministry: the giving of sight to the man born blind (John 9); the healing of the paralytic (Mark 2), and the Sermon on the Mount (Matthew 5). The journey of Jesus takes a turn on Palm Sunday (Mark 11) when triumph quickly turns, first to betrayal (Mark 14) and then to mockery and condemnation (Mark 15). The final steps of the journey mirror the lonely beginnings in Eden as, all alone, Jesus carries the cross to the hill of Calvary where deadly wood will become the Tree of Life (Mark 15).

The culmination of the great procession of the two Testaments is the heavenly Jerusalem, depicted in the rounded tympanum above the center doors. Here, the victorious Lamb of God reigns over the holy city with its twelve gates facing east, north, south and west (Revelation 21).

The waters which brought life and deliverance all along the journey of both Old and New Testaments (the rivers of Eden, the waters of the Great Flood, the Red Sea, the River Jordan) have now become *"the river of life-giving water, clear as crystal, which issues from the throne of God and the Lamb,"* watering the trees of life *"whose leaves serve for the healing of the nations"* (Revelation 22).

The cast bronze door stoppers relate two stories from the gospels. The two outer stops, the cock and the apostle Peter, bring to mind Peter's denial of Jesus before the cock crowed, and the bitter tears he later shed. The two inner door stops, St. James the Apostle and the fish, call to mind the calling of this patron of the cathedral, who left his father, his fishing, and his nets to follow Jesus. ❏

The healing of the sick.   *The Sermon on the Mount.*

Riding to Jerusalem.

Alone, Jesus carries the cross to Calvary.

The tympanum above the center doors depicts the culmination of the great procession of the two testaments. The Lamb of God reigns over the holy city within the gates of Heaven.

Door stop: Peter weeps.

The life-giving water, issuing from the lamb, heals the nations.

IN THE HEART OF THE CITY

by David Brewster

Back in 1994, I received an invitation from Father Michael G. Ryan, the pastor of St. James, to tour his pride (if priests can have pride) and joy: the renovations-in-progress of St. James Cathedral. Sounded interesting, though I went with a fairly high degree of skepticism.

Architects were there, pointing out the gilding of the Corinthian columns then under way. I was given a complete acoustical lecture, explaining how the tiles had been peeled from the ceiling and replaced with coffered boxes to disperse the formerly boomy sound. The pastor went into raptures over the progress of the carving of the *ambo* (pulpit) by a New York artist who was setting Isaiah 55: 10-11 into wood. (That's a passage about the divine word going forth like Northwest rainstorms.) I was soon getting dizzy with stories of new bells, stained glass windows coming out of hiding, the *oculus* that let sunlight down onto the new central altar.

I was stunned. An institution that I had put off in a secondary corner of my mind was coming back to extraordinary life, shedding a rather worn carapace in hopes of emerging as one of the most vital and beautiful Catholic cathedrals in the nation. And in Seattle, of all cities.

Not that Seattle does not sometimes pull off these feats of rediscovery. An earlier secular saint, Victor Steinbrueck (who always reminded me of Archbishop Raymond Hunthausen, his contemporary, for his stubborn idealism), made the town see that there was beauty in the neglected buildings of Pioneer Square and a kind of urban soul in the rundown Pike Place Market. Dean John Leffler of St. Mark's Episcopal Cathedral arrived in 1951 to find a classic half-finished Seattle project (whose unbuilt 250-foot tower recalls the St. James' collapsed dome). In a formula that somewhat prefigures that at St. James, Dean Leffler insisted on fine music, opened up the church to the creative currents on Capitol Hill, and stirred the embers with some bold political stands.

When I woke up to the story of St. James on that lovely fall day in 1994, it is fair to say that I was struggling to emerge from a profound ignorance of the cathedral and Catholic life in Seattle. The city was very middle class and Protestant, which gave Catholicism a kind of secondary place in local affairs, or so I thought. The cathedral had poor acoustics, and I remember going to weddings or other events there and spending a lot of time gazing upward, not in spiritual rapture but to deplore the acoustical tiles on the ceiling. It seemed like a place whose best days were behind it.

As I began to spend more time at the cathedral, especially drawn by the marvelous music that now bloomed in its splendor, I started to understand its remarkable and dramatic story. This saga is, in its way, very emblematic of Seattle's own history. It's a story of grand initial ambitions, serious setbacks, uncertain first steps at renewal, and then the happy discovery of the formula for realizing those early, glorious hopes.

The annual Corpus Christi procession begins as altar servers lead the congregation out of the cathedral and onto the surrounding Seattle streets. The photos accompanying this essay are of the 1999 Corpus Christi procession.

Just down my street in Madrona is the house where Mary McCarthy spent some of her rebellious adolescent years, with her grandparents, the Prestons. Nothing (save boys) seemed to please her, but among her barbed remarks about her "Catholic girlhood" is her sense that, for all she deplored about a Catholic education, at least it gave one a tragic sense of life, a consciousness, rare for Americans outside the South, "of being on the losing side." This gave a special urgency, a narrative line, to one's life, she wrote.

Seattle is sometimes described as the least Catholic large American city outside the South, so the odds of building a great cathedral here must have seemed appallingly long from the first. Perhaps that's why St. James overreached—putting up the famous dome that fell in 1916 from too much snow (in Seattle!)—and struggled to keep the grand space heated during the Depression. The ambitious music program started by Dr. Franklin Palmer declined. There was a rebirth during the years of Archbishop Thomas Connolly, 1948-75, when the cathedral was refurbished and dozens of schools, convents, and churches were built. But then another decline set in as the number of women entering the teaching orders and men entering the priesthood dropped so sharply that many parish schools had to be closed. Meanwhile, the neighborhood around St. James became poorer and more impacted by the expansion of First Hill's hospitals. Seattle's first great suburb, blessed with fine homes, churches, clubs, and apartment hotels that enjoyed grand views from the promontory, was treated badly by a noisy freeway, all those hospitals, and other institutions that crowded out the residential life.

One legacy of the Second Vatican Council of 1962 was to downplay cathedrals, in order to stress parish life. Given all these factors, St. James of the early 1970's was a troubled institution. The parish on First Hill had become quite small. The cathedral building itself attracted priests and others fond of grand ceremonial

moments, but the parish was becoming inward, with a modest community profile, and short on funds for its music budgets. When James Savage, then a music teacher and conductor, was approached about becoming the director of music at St. James, he called up a fellow conductor who told him St. James was "a black hole" for a musician. "Why would you consider it?" she inquired. And yet, it was the right moment. Savage has made a tremendous success of the cathedral musically, turning it into one of the finest in the nation.

As that story suggests, St. James' low point was actually more of a turning point. Vatican II may have downplayed cathedrals, but it also released enormous vitalizing energies by opening the Church to pluralism, shared governance, and a greater role for the individual conscience. Archbishop Hunthausen fully embodied this new spirit, earning an appellation as "the quintessential Vatican II bishop" (*Washingtonians*, page 477). The Church was being redefined from being about law and discipline into "the whole people of God," where personal experience and the spirit of love were being given new sanction. Much of this was to find expression in Hunthausen and, later, in the plans for recasting the shape and feel of St. James' building.

If Bishop O'Dea was the great envisioner of the grand cathedral, Archbishop Hunthausen may well have been its savior, despite the turbulent period of his administration. Almost by accident, Hunthausen put the archdiocese on the world map (and vividly in Seattle's awareness) when he withheld taxes to protest nuclear weapons, permitted Dignity, an organization of Catholic gay people, to celebrate a Mass at St. James in 1983, and came close to advocating unilateral nuclear disarmament by America. An agony of interventions from Rome, shared authority, and hard feelings resulted. Careers were derailed, with Hunthausen's trusted and effective heir-apparent, Michael Ryan, deflected from administration and shifted to become pastor of the cathedral. Father Ryan, in turn, had the organizational ability and architectural vision to turn into reality Hunthausen's dream for a renovated and outwardly-turned St. James. The spirit of Vatican II moves in mysterious ways.

One vivid example of rebirth is with the music and liturgy program. When Savage joined the cathedral it was a time when Seattle arts were starting to take off, and he was looking for a way to be a part of the excitement. He befriended a monk, Brother Elias, who urged Savage to help revive the musical traditions of St. James and to meet the cathedral's pastor, Father William E. Gallagher. In July, 1981, Savage took a mighty leap of faith and signed on as director of music.

He discovered that the cathedral had a grand tradition in music, right from the start. Dr. Palmer, a skin doctor, had become "Mr. Music" in early Seattle as a co-founder of the Symphony, music director at Temple de Hirsch, violist, and passionate lover of organ music. He started with a magnificent organ in the west gallery, a Hutchings-Votey from the noted Boston firm. Palmer had studied organ in France and he favored French organ music, then flourishing. The Hutchings-Votey was designed for a time when organs would play symphonic transcriptions. They were noted for their many voices which resembled symphony instruments and the smooth progression of sonorities and dynamics they could produce, like an orchestra. By now, the Hutchings-Votey is back in

A child swings her ribbons in glee as she tags along with her mother in the choir.

The men of the Cathedral Choir play their part.

favor, a monument of an instrument, but in 1981, the clear, lean Baroque style was in fashion and the organ seemed another obstacle to be overcome.

But the cathedral of Dr. Palmer, who had a fatal heart attack at the organ keyboard on Palm Sunday in 1934, had laid the foundations for much that would be revived in the 1980s and in the renovated cathedral of the 1990s. Dr. Palmer planned an echo organ for the dome area which was eventually located in the east nave. (That organ was replaced in 1999 by the Thomas J. Murphy Millennium organ.) The second organ was there to permit works for two organs and to accompany the excellent men's choir of his day. That choir, augmented by a boys' choir from the Cathedral School, spread the cathedral's fame through radio broadcasts, starting in 1922. It was known for its singing of Gregorian chant, now gloriously revived in Seattle.

Much of what Dr. Palmer started fell apart during the Depression and after his death. Once it weathered financial hard times, the cathedral then seemed headed for the fate of many such grand structures in America: a small parish, open primarily for ceremonial occasions and for visitors, too short on funds for much musical excellence. But Father Gallagher, together with his new director, had a plan to avoid that fate. A storage area in the rectory basement was turned into a parish center. Ice cream socials began to rebuild community and to tie together the poorer neighborhoods to the south of St. James with the society homes to the north. The lovely gardens surrounding the campus were revived.

Savage set to work on the musical renaissance. Neither organ was fully working, and during one performance of a Mozart Mass, when the Casavant organ in the east nave failed, a pump organ had to be wheeled in for emergency use. Savage put an ad in The Seattle *Weekly* for good singers and called in all his chits to cobble together a choir of 35. He put on the first concert in 40 years. He started inviting local instrumental

Altar ministers, bearing an historic banner, escort the Blessed Sacrament beneath the canopy.

ensembles and choruses to become resident companies at the cathedral, practicing there, performing at the cathedral and in other parishes, putting on a concert each year. All these initiatives were to bear bountiful fruit, and today St. James is bursting with choral excellence, has an active children's music program for 85 children and an advanced *Schola Cantorum* for 24 young people. The organ has been repaired, and the cathedral has two distinguished full-time organists to cope with the 600 services a year, each with at least one professional singer and an organist.

One of Dr. Savage's notable ideas was a program of Great Music for Great Cathedrals, which he started in 1983 as a way of celebrating music written for cathedrals or influenced by them. It has become a huge draw, a richly splendid, dramatically lighted and staged extravaganza that is St. James' calling card to Seattle's musical community and a display of the cathedral's extraordinary musical resources. But if the cathedral has been able to revive traditions of pomp and sensuous ceremony, it has also benefited from the revival of early music performance practice in Seattle. Savage loves to tell the story of the time he was considering how to replace a guitar Mass that had been meant to attract younger people. His idea was to go "clear the other way," by doing Gregorian chant with a women's choir (since St. Mark's had staked a claim for a medieval men's choir with its Compline Choir), complete with full vestments and processions. Attendance went up sharply, particularly among young people. Everyone who auditioned for the choir was under 30, Savage was amazed to find. Still unbelieving, he explained to one young woman that the music would have no guitars and derived from medieval musical traditions, that grand thousand years of Western music that underlay the music of the last 400 years. "Great!" replied the woman. "Finally something for us young people."

The culmination of all this musical rebirth was the redesign of the cathedral for better acoustics. The main step was to replace the acoustical tiles on the ceiling with coffered elements to break up the reflections, rather than trying to absorb them. The result is a very rich, cathedral sound, with a decay time (or ring time) of five to six seconds, a heart-stopping diminuendo into infinity that is perfectly even across the voices as it fades. The first goal was to enhance congregational singing so that an individual singer hears himself clearly while also sensing the massed voices of others. "You don't feel alone," explains Savage. "You are adding something." (I tried it, and he's right.)

The achievement is all the more remarkable when one considers the difficulty church music has experienced in recent decades. English cathedrals still have endowments to support their musical traditions, but American ones have had to struggle against the tide. "Jim brought it back from zero," marvels one appreciator of organ and choral music in Seattle. Audiences for organ concerts continue to decline. Against this, St. James is a vital center of Seattle's musical life, presenting its programs with high professionalism and careful attention to liturgical traditions while experimenting with modern liturgical practices by virtue of its reconfigured worship space, and always making programs freely available to the poor.

Seattle is a city of hills, but it is curious how few of them have a crowning structure atop them, unless you consider television broadcast towers in that category. But St. James always has crowned First Hill, and in the old photographs, when the city was low rise and St. James had its famous high dome, it truly dominated the city. As of course cathedrals did in history.

The women of the Cathedral Choir lead the people in song.

They were among the mightiest and most beautiful and most comprehensive achievements of mankind.

St. James' pastor, Father Michael G. Ryan, not only spent several years in Rome, where he studied at the Jesuits' Gregorian University and was ordained a priest at St. Peter's, but he has become something of a scholar of cathedrals. Before taking up his post at St. James, he spent two months touring English cathedrals, pondering their greatness, worrying about their diminished vitality. He says he was struck by the way cathedrals served their time as public squares and stages. Mystery plays arose in them, giving a kind of birth to theater. Universities had their origins around them. Market places crowded up against them, and the business of the day would spill noisily inside them before Mass or when it rained. They sheltered the poor, on whose faces God is said to be most easily seen. They were mother and teacher, "*Mater et Magistra.*" They sprang from a time, "a hot moment," Edith Hamilton called them, when patrons, artists, and audience seemed to coalesce around a grand enterprise. Intellectual, artistic, religious life all found a center, a unified sensibility.

St. James, with its block-long edifice, commanding location, fine renaissance-revival architecture must have seemed heartbreakingly capable of such a unification of life. It had "good bones," Ryan likes to say, though many of them had been covered over with designs that no longer worked well. Yet the old place was dearly loved by families that had built it, decorated it, worshipped in it. Changing it would not be easy.

From Archbishop Hunthausen he learned the importance of "how you tell your story." That meant capitalizing on some big splashes like Great Music for Great Cathedrals to draw in a public that had forgotten about St. James. It meant using the cathedral as an ecumenical gathering place at moments of great civic urgency, such as the prayer vigils during the Gulf War. It meant attracting worshippers from farther away than the local parish, using with great care and skill the grand and glorious liturgy of the Roman Church. It meant being more welcoming than the somewhat upper-crusty cathedral of recent reputation. It meant paying more attention to the needs of an increasingly poor neighborhood by doing more for the homeless, enhancing an extensive program to teach English as a second language for refugees and immigrants, and encouraging letter-writing campaigns for better housing, health care and nutrition.

The new pastor began the custom of inviting 30 or 40 Seattle notables to come to the music, with a little reception before and after when Father Ryan, with his fine Irish sense of just the right little pleasantry for each person (and a politician's great memory for names), would circulate cheerfully. And with his great dream of a revived, renovated cathedral, Father Ryan also knew the importance of timing—letting the congregation participate in the new design, allowing a decent interval to pass from the previous regime.

Finally, the moment was right for dramatic change, starting about a decade ago. Father Ryan had in mind a new orientation of the Church, a place of exchange like the crossroads of an urban center. In spirit, this owed much to Vatican II, being more about pluralism and love

The choir kneels for Benediction of the Blessed Sacrament in the courtyard of O'Dea High School.

The people gather in the courtyard.

than about the more rigid and doctrinal side of the Church. And soon he was to find this spirit made physical, in the architectural bones of the old building.

The story of the discovery of the key to the building, and this spiritual reawakening, has elements of the uncanny. A liturgical design consultant, Rev. Richard Vosko, excitedly approached Father Ryan one Sunday after Mass with the discovery that the center of the building lay right under the crossing, despite the illusion from the long arcades that the crossing under the former dome seemed much closer to the east altar than to the western doors. Father Ryan later reinforced this discovery himself when an old newspaper article from the Seattle *Times* of 1905 surfaced, saying that the distinguished New York architectural firm of Heins and La Farge (architects of St. John the Divine in New York and St. Matthew's Cathedral in DC) had intended to locate the altar directly beneath the great dome. Suddenly the building had declared its inmost essence, and the renovation project seemed more properly described as a restoration.

Other discoveries followed, such as the inlaid mosaic floors underneath all that drab carpeting and some stained-glass windows that had been plastered over. But the key was putting the altar on a raised circle right in the center of St. James. It meant that the bishop and the pastor sat among their people, not on a distant, royal throne. It meant nearly all the congregation were close to the action, no longer looking at the backs of heads, but across the grand central space with its glowing white eucharistic table, at each other, at faces of "the whole people of God." Anchoring that sense of centering is the new *oculus*, letting sunlight down onto that central space and ringed with Christ's words: *"I am in your midst as one who serves."*

I wandered up to St. James the other day, late on a sunny spring Sunday, arriving a half hour before Mass was to begin. As the cathedral began to fill up, I could sense how much of this vision was actually happening. There was a growing hum of conversation as people circulated and greeted each other, just as they might in an Italian piazza. People entered from four sides of the central "square," spotting each other or a priest and moving to have a word together. And it was theatrical as ministers set out objects for worship, adjusted microphones, went "backstage" to get ready.

Taking a seat in the east nave, I watch as glints of sunlight play around the interior space, the east apse windows glowing an almost-Chartres blue in the bright late afternoon. Father Ryan spots me and drops by to explain that the stained-glass actually looks best when not in direct sunlight, citing his good friend, Hans Gottfried von Stockhausen, the renowned German stained-glass artist who completely re-created the three east windows now emerging in full glory from years behind the Casavant organ. I marvel again at the windows and then notice how the eye is drawn, rayed outward as it were, constantly away from a simple axis and up the ribs of the vaulting or outward into the north and south apses. The space has a baroque splendor and ripeness, but it is almost bound into a unity. It makes, for Seattle, a pleasing complement to St. Mark's, with its rough-hewn and boldly unfinished look, for St. James now seems, nearly a century after Bishop O'Dea's amazing vision for it, a very finished and glowing jewel.

But of course it is not finished, as Father Ryan's homily that afternoon tried to explain. He urged the congregation to think well of Doubting Thomas, who asked hard questions of Jesus and his fellow apostles, for being human meant asking questions, worrying about the glaring imperfections of the Church, which he described as a "perfectly imperfect" institution, one that is tarnished yet divine. Do not muffle your tough questions, he said, whether they be about the Church's changing too fast, or too slowly, about sexual ethics, about the role of women, about gays, about divorce, about sexual abuse among the clergy.

Walking around the campus of the cathedral, as I did recently with Father Ryan, is to be struck by how perfectly imperfect its whole story has been. We began in the rectory, where he has his rather splendid office. One small room, now a reception area, used to house all the business of the chancery, he says. Across the street, where now there is a convent for the Sisters of Holy Names, used to be the Frye mansion (home of the family that endowed the Frye Museum) now handsomely expanded. We look into the Cathedral Place Hall, originally a Catholic school but now used as a cafeteria for O'Dea students at lunch and the homeless at dinner. Upstairs are classrooms for ESL instruction and a large, very well used choir rehearsal room. Music has always been a part of Father Ryan's life, he observes in passing. He took piano from age 6 and became enough of an amateur organist to dream about playing a hymn on the new organ in the east nave.

We're back outside on Terry and looking at the Gothic facade of O'Dea, a high school famous for its plucky sports teams. Down the street is the Brothers' residence, where the teachers of O'Dea live, and next door, in

The parishioners, spilling out of the courtyard, proclaim their faith to the city at large.

a modest First Hill home that recalls the grand past, lives an old gentleman, Mr. Brown, who occasionally encounters the pastor on his walk and tells him he can still remember seeing Bishop O'Dea walk those same sidewalks.

We pause outside the cathedral, O'Dea's monument on the hill. He had always felt it was a notable piece of design, Father Ryan says. He alludes to Bramante's Renaissance churches, like Santa Maria della Consolazione in Todi, Italy, that were built around a central altar, as a sign of the historical depth of the new design. But mostly he is simply grateful for the way the reborn St. James has changed its community, helped it escape from "the anonymous feeling of looking at all those backs of heads," made it, through architecture, "more aware of being a community."

As we part, we look up. A long white rope is floating down from one of the towers, where masonry cleaners are at work. It is a reminder, on that day with spring coming on after a very dark Seattle winter, of how high St. James has aspired, of how, even when it was cast down, a rope was always there to pull it back up, and of how the work—which seems so gloriously consummated and radiantly fulfilled—goes on.❏

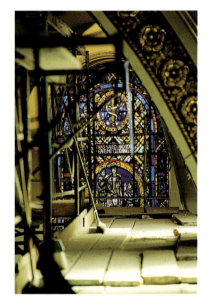

Interior view of the south window in the east apse
when work was underway during the 1994 renovation

David Brewster is a Seattle journalist and founded the Seattle Weekly.
He currently writes a column for the Seattle Times *and is executive*
director of Town Hall, a community cultural center on First Hill.
Brewster has lived in Seattle for 34 years.

a place of Prayer & Protest

神戸の人々のために祈ります

Father Richard Ward lights a candle for the victims of the 1995 earthquake in Kobe, Japan.

St. James is a gathering place for people of all faiths in times of international crisis or natural disaster, in times of anxiety and sorrow.

Before the statue of the Blessed Virgin Mary, Tim Jovanovich bowed his head in prayer for his homeland, war-torn Bosnia-Herzegovina, in February, 1994. "From all the ends of the world, we bring you our suffering," he prayed softly.

Jovanovich's prayer has joined hundreds of thousands of others prayed at St. James Cathedral for almost a century. Masses and prayer services here continually help those who gather to share the pain and sorrow felt at the heart of tragedies that take place a world away.

In recent years prayers were sent heavenward to a haunting melody from a traditional flute in response to a massive, deadly earthquake in Kobe, Japan. Tens of thousands marched from the steps of the cathedral to protest the Gulf War, and people of all faiths and from Seattle's diverse communities gathered as brothers and sisters to pray for the assassinated Prime Minister of Israel, Yitzhak Rabin.

Those who gather at St. James Cathedral to pray or protest transcend the crisis at hand and come closer to God.

"How good it is to come together as brothers and sisters."

Remembering the Holocaust *April, 1997*

Proving that the memory of the Holocaust lives on in their generation, hundreds of Seattle children from area Jewish and Christian congregations, elementary schools and high schools, gathered at St. James for prayer and remembrance of the Holocaust which included readings and dramatizations by the young people, a candle-lighting ceremony and the sounding of the *Shofar* (ram's horn).

Assassinated Prime Minister of Israel *November, 1995*

Following an interfaith service at St. James to remember the assassinated Prime Minister of Israel Yitzhak Rabin, an editorial appeared in the Seattle *Times* which read: "During these days of shock and grief…the outpouring of support and expressions of condolence from Seattle's diverse communities has been profound. Standing with other religious and civic leaders, and joined by a thousand people at St. James Cathedral on Monday night, the words of a Hebrew prayer filled the void which death imparts: 'How good it is to come together as brothers and sisters.'"

Left: The Shofar *is sounded at a remembrance service for the Holocaust.*
Below left: The sound of traditional Japanese songs eased the anxieties of many who gathered to pray for the victims of an earthquake in Kobe, Japan, 1995.
Center: Mourning mother and daughter pray for four fallen Seattle firefighters at a Taizé-inspired prayer service.
Below right: Following a Mass for Peace, a couple stops to pray for victims of the Bosnian war at a temporary shrine in the Cathedral Chapel.

In 1991, thirty thousand marchers flowed from St. James Cathedral through Seattle's streets to protest the Gulf War.

While covering this event, the local NBC affiliate, KING TV, called St. James Cathedral *"Seattle's place to grieve."*

Desert Storm *January, 1991*

Police estimated over 30,000 people gathered at St. James to march for peace in the Middle East on January 14, 1991. Toddlers and the elderly, Protestants, Catholics, Jews and Muslims, yuppies and anarchists took to the streets of Seattle to protest the Gulf War. Marching with clasped hands, singing and chanting and moving as if they were one large family, the crowd flowed from St. James across Capitol Hill to St. Mark's Episcopal Cathedral.

The Death of Four Firefighters *January, 1995*

At an emotional service for four fallen Seattle firemen, uniformed firefighters dotted the crowd. Only the chattering of small children broke the weighty silence in the nave as over a thousand people gathered in candlelight. The sound of the children was a reminder of the families the four brave firefighters left behind.

Colorado High School Shootings *April, 1999*

The nation was stunned after thirteen youths were gunned down at Columbine High School in Littleton, Colorado. That week, the cathedral was filled with Seattle school students attending a Mass to pray for the victims. Many of the students brought bouquets of flowers and placed them before an outdoor shrine of Mary holding the Child Jesus. ❑

Archbishop Thomas J. Murphy and Father Michael G. Ryan pray before a temporary shrine dedicated to victims of the Oklahoma City bombing, April, 1995.

a place to Sing

God's Praises

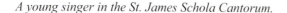

A young singer in the St. James Schola Cantorum.

A t St. James Cathedral God brings disparate people together and makes them a single body with one praying voice. At Mass throughout the weekend, when the Our Father is sung in the nave, the sound renders St. James as Church at its most human, yet most splendid: the Holy Spirit manifest.

I am a cathedral parishioner. I have worshipped in many places, from European cathedrals to rural parishes and monasteries. I came upon St. James in the 1970's and since then, it has been my spiritual home. I serve in the choir, in the religious education program and as a reader at Mass.

For me, this cathedral has realized the liturgical vision of the Second Vatican Council in a powerful way to the joy of its people. Those who come to a liturgy or a concert simply get hooked. If they are not Catholic, they may seek out the RCIA; if they are, they often join the cathedral parish, even if it means taking a ferry across Puget Sound every Sunday.

We love the pealing bronze bells and the grandeur of the Hutchings-Votey, a concert organ in the finest tradition of the turn of the 20th Century, and the new Rosales Millennium organ in its classic tradition. We love the many fine choirs: the children's choirs, the Women of St. James Schola, the adult mixed choir, not to mention the visiting choirs and choruses in residence. Here, there is a sense that there is something worthy of our deepest human aspirations.

And we love the solemnities: the Corpus Christi procession, popular in the best sense of the word, the Easter Vigil with the Word proclaimed in near darkness (and where candles really shine), the solemn return of the Paschal *alleluia* intoned by our archbishop, and the joyful anticipation of the neophytes eager to be anointed with sweet chrism.

We love the special liturgies of Ordination, the Chrism Mass, the Rite of Election, when people from throughout the archdiocese gather as one Church and observe a thanksgiving which makes and keeps us one.

We love the many musical concerts which enrich our city's life and to which the poor are always welcome free of charge. The poor are a part of the inner life of the cathedral, and here they are gladly received and treated with the dignity they deserve. *Everyone* is welcome because all are called to this wonderful feast of good things for the soul, a sign of the great abundance of the reign of God.

Thomas Stratman

the Cathedral Choirs

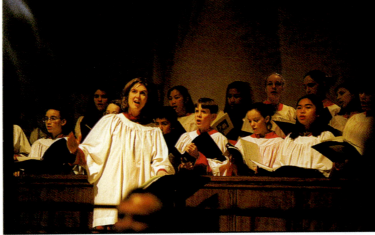

Previous page: *The Women of St. James Schola sings before Midnight Mass on Christmas Eve.* **Top left:** *Cathedral Psalmists lead the congregation at each of the five Sunday Masses.* **Left:** *The St. James Schola Cantorum is one of the cathedral's three children's choirs.*

Above: *The Cathedral Choir sings the national anthem at the opening of a Seattle Mariners' baseball game, 1996. Proceeds for the game went to Catholic Community Services of Western Washington. This volunteer choir has toured Italy singing in major cathedrals, and through Russia just before the collapse of the Soviet Union.*
Right: *A scene from "Great Music for Great Cathedrals," a popular performance staged annually, presenting centuries of sacred music composed for cathedrals around the world.*

Center: *Cathedral soloists accompany the all-parish choir which sings at Sunday Mass in the summer months while the Cathedral Choir takes a summer break.* **Above:** *View of the men of the Cathedral Choir singing in the high gallery above the west nave with the Hutchings-Votey organ pipes behind them, Midnight Mass, Christmas Eve, 1998. The Cathedral Choir's recorded compact disk has sold nationwide to the acclaim of national critics.*

Above: Dr. James Savage, director of Music and Liturgy, reverences the altar with the Women of St. James Schola.
Right: The cathedral choir supports the singing ministers and assembly at Midnight Mass on Christmas. Archbishop Alexander J. Brunett presides.

"The choristers of St. James minister as servants and priests, supporting the congregation, leading them in song." — *Dr. James Savage*

Every Sunday, following the preface to the Eucharistic Prayer at Mass, the presider proclaims: *"…and so with all the choirs of angels we proclaim your glory and join in their unending hymn of praise."* In response, the congregation sings in acclamation: *"Holy, holy, holy Lord, God of power and might, heaven and earth are full of your glory. Hosanna in the highest."*

The many choirs of St. James who join the angels to sing God's praises include the "choir" of the people assembled, the ministers who serve at the altar, and the voices, strings, bells and brass of the cathedral music program. In over 600 liturgies every year, one, all, or a combination of choirs sing out with the congregation in joyous acclamation: the **Cathedral Choir** (a 60-member choir); the **Women of St.**

James Schola; the **Psalmists** who proclaim the Word and lead the assembly in its response; the **Cathedral Cantorei** (professional soloists and cantors); the three children's choirs: the **St. Gregory Choir** (the littlest ones), the **St. Cecilia Choir** (older children), and the **Schola Cantorum**; the **Cathedral Chamber Orchestra** and the **Cathedral Brass**; and the **Cathedral Pipers** (an ensemble of up to 16).

Every year St. James' music program presents performances by many multi-cultural visiting choirs and the cathedral's own resident choirs. An annual season of concerts is also presented, and includes *Great Music for Great Cathedrals*, an enormously popular evening of staged sacred music composed through the centuries for the world's great cathedrals.

the Cathedral Bells

Cathedral bells are the voice of the church in the city, singing out praises in joyful celebration and tolling tones of sorrow in times of tragedy.

During the 1960's, an electronic carillon was installed in the cathedral's north tower. For the next thirty years people were summoned to prayer by the amplified electronic sound of bells.

The carillon was destroyed by a fire in March, 1992. Since the 1994 renovation, St. James Cathedral has a six-bell peal of authentic bronze bells, cast for the cathedral in Holland. Each bell was named and blessed in a celebration which was held in the summer of 1994.

In accordance with Catholic tradition, two bells were named for clergy serving at the time of their blessing and installation. "Thomas" was named for Archbishop Thomas J. Murphy, "Michael," for the cathedral's pastor, Father Michael G. Ryan.

The bells are laid along the street before the blessing ceremony in the summer of 1994.

The bells are blessed in a celebration on the cathedral grounds.

Another of the bells, "James," is named for the cathedral's patron saint, and a fourth, "Francesca," for St. Frances X. Cabrini. Mother Cabrini was America's first canonized saint and lived in Seattle during the early years of the 20th century.

There is a bell named "Raymond" in honor of Archbishop Raymond G. Hunthausen and another, "Anthony," in honor of St. Anthony of Padua.

The bells hang in the cathedral's south tower beside "Our Lady of Good Help." For nearly eighty years this pioneer bell rang from the belfry of Seattle's first Catholic church, Our Lady of Good Help, until that church, located at Fifth Avenue and Jefferson Street, was razed.

The bell's gentle tones, summoned by the pulling of a rope, are suited to a country village. "Our Lady" was the first bell ever to ring in the tower of a Catholic church in the city of Seattle, and it now rings with those newly-cast for St. James.

Depending on the day's humidity and the direction and speed of the wind, the sounds of St. James' bells can be heard throughout downtown Seattle.

The pioneer bell, "Our Lady of Good Help," was the first to ring from a Catholic church in Seattle.

Workers secure the ropes before hoisting the 2,000 pound "Thomas" bell to St. James' south tower.

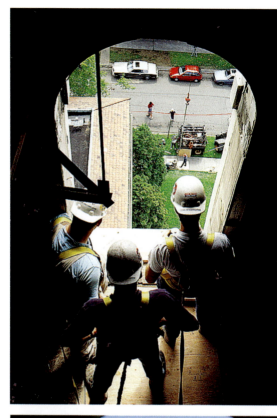

Top left: *Workers wait in the belfry for the first bell to be raised by pulleys.* **Top center:** *A bell is lifted over the heads of the workers.* **Top right:** *The first bell meets the tower.* **Lower right:** *The bell is secured before hanging.* **Center:** *Workers prepare the second bell to be raised and hung.* **Lower center:** *View of four of the six bells hanging in the south tower. "Our Lady of Good Help" (front right) is operated by a rope. The new bells, the largest of which weighs 2,000 pounds and is 4 feet in diameter, are struck by hammers activated by an electronic clock. The peals can be pre-programmed or the bells can be rung manually. The "Michael" bell is front left; behind it is "Francesca." Sections of the "Thomas," "James" and "Anthony" bells can be seen as well.* **Bottom left:** *View of the south tower from the north tower's belfry.*

The cathedral bells sing out in praise announcing Masses, weddings and great events, and they toll at funerals. They also ring at noon each day and at six o'clock in the evening for the Angelus, the prayer commemorating the angel Gabriel's announcement to the Blessed Virgin Mary that she would give birth to the Christ.

the **Cathedral Organs**

The Archbishop Thomas J. Murphy Millennium Organ.
Dr. James Savage directs the Cathedral Choir, Chamber
Orchestra and Brass.

"Let every instrument be tuned for praise!"

Organs have been used in liturgical worship since at least the tenth century. St. James Cathedral has four organs to accompany and enrich liturgical song. They are also featured in concerts of sacred music: the *Archbishop Thomas J. Murphy Organ,* the *west gallery* organ, the *Corpus Christi* organ and the *portative* organ.

The *Archbishop Thomas J. Murphy Millennium Organ* was built by Manuel Rosales Organ Builders of Los Angeles in 1999. It consists of 48 ranks of pipes over three manual divisions and pedals. Five of those ranks have been incorporated from the 1926 Casavant organ which stood behind St. James' old high altar in the east apse. The new organ was carefully designed to provide musical leadership to accompany cathedral choral ensembles and support a more authentic performance of baroque music for liturgies and concerts. A four-manual master console allows a single organist complete control over the tonal resources of both the Rosales organ and the Hutchings-Votey in the west gallery.

The *Hutchings-Votey* organ, built by the prestigious Boston organ-builder George Hutchings, has graced St. James' west gallery since the opening of the cathedral in 1907. Virtually unplayable by the 1970's, this massive organ has undergone extensive restoration. The restoration of the cathedral itself in 1994 provided acoustics which revealed a tonal opulence in this organ which had been hidden for nearly fifty years. The console was then restored in 1997, and today this organ stands as a noteworthy representative of the finest craftsmanship of its period. "The Hutchings-Votey is one of the few large, turn-of-the-century organs still in existence in this country," says cathedral organist Joseph Adam, "and lends particular authenticity to the performance of music from the Romantic era."

The *portative* organ, built by Laukhuff/Zukerman in 1981, consists of three ranks of pipes with divided stops for great flexibility. A keyboard-shift mechanism allows instant transposition down one semi-tone. This small compact, portable organ is used for liturgies and concerts in both the Cathedral Chapel and the cathedral itself.

The medieval replica organ, *Corpus Christi*, was built by Frans Bosman of Portland, Oregon, in 1984 and includes three ranks of copper pipes and a set of hand-cast German bronze bells. The organ requires two players for performance: one to draw the sliders, located under each note (a precursor to the more familiar keyboard), the second to supply wind through two wedge bellows. This organ is used in the performance of medieval liturgical music. It was bequeathed to the cathedral by Howard Hoyt, cathedral organist for seventeen years.

Under the GREAT central DOME

by Stephen Lee

Cathedrals have always been at the heart of the city and have reflected the religious values and attitudes of the communities they serve. They are places of worship and the performing arts, providing spiritual and cultural identity and civic pride. For architects, they have always presented the greatest of opportunities and challenges, demanding a balance between aesthetic awareness and theological acumen.

The word *cathedral* may conjure up an image of tradition and stability, but cathedrals change with the times in response to the changing society around them. Even the use of pews instead of chairs for the new St. James Cathedral was thought a modern idea at the turn of the century!

Ecclesiastical architecture has always been affected both by the aesthetic, technical and political thinking of the day and by the contemporary understanding of the Kingdom of God. The earliest Christians simply gathered in one another's homes around an ordinary table, recalling the Last Supper. Eucharist was also celebrated at the burial tombs of Christian martyrs, known as *martyria*.

Architect Stephen Lee (center) discusses coffering with plaster artisans.

Design of St. James Cathedral, 1906, by architects Heins and La Farge.

These early forms of centralized assembly were common until the Peace of Milan in AD 313 established the civil legitimacy of Christianity. From that point on the basilica, or Roman meeting house, was integrated with the martyrium-altar. So began the development of the traditional nave-plan that evolved into the great Gothic cathedrals of western Europe.

A Living Composition

Great cathedrals typically embody a wonderful living composition of architectural and liturgical practices of succeeding generations. St. James Cathedral is no exception.

The word *cathedral* may conjure up an image of tradition and stability, but cathedrals change with the times in response to the changing society around them.

This piece of the sanctuary floor, which read VENITE ADOREMUS, was nearly destroyed in the 1950 renovation and has been recreated and placed at the entrance to the Blessed Sacrament Chapel.

1907

The elegant Neo-Italian Renaissance exterior of St. James Cathedral, built in 1907, was originally designed with a simple interior by the New York architects Heins and La Farge (original architects for St. John the Divine in New York).

1916 and 1950

The large central dome subsequently collapsed in a 1916 snow storm, which gave local architect John Graham an opportunity to reorder the layout and completely decorate the interior in the Corinthian plaster detailing that we see today. Four large corner piers were introduced at the crossing in order to support a new central dome, a dome that was never built. In 1950 the interior was redecorated in the eclectic style of that age under the direction of the Rambusch Studio, again of New York, in collaboration with local architect John Maloney.

1994

The most recent renovation of St. James Cathedral, by Bumgardner Architects of Seattle (1994), has given this era its own opportunity to make new again this historic building. The overriding goal was to incorporate the teachings of the Second Vatican Council (1962 to 1965) and change the focus of liturgical action to the midst of the assembly. This was achieved, in large part, by moving the altar to the center of the space.

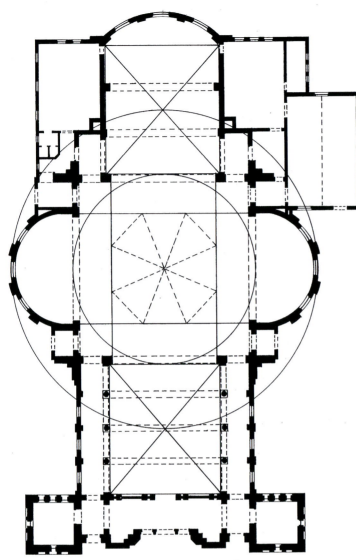

Interior floor plan by New York
architectural firm Heins and La Farge (1907).
The circular lines show underlying renaissance
proportions of the cathedral plan.

The architectural theorists of the Italian Renaissance, Alberti, Bramante, Michelangelo and Palladio (circa 1330 to 1600) based their designs on classical Greek and Roman architecture. They looked upon architecture as an art form with beauty of design as the predominant idea. Indeed, many were painters and sculptors as well as architects. In the design of churches they were intrigued with creating buildings based on the laws of geometry that, to them, symbolized the perfect nature of God. The Renaissance plan is based on a return to the early Christian concept of the centralized form, the altar centered below a circular dome within a square building. This juxtaposition of the square, a human invention depicting material space on its periphery, with the circle, a metaphor for the divine without beginning or end, focuses upon a timeless center: the altar!

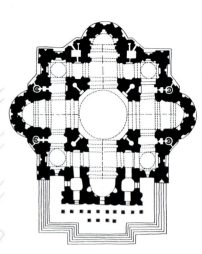

This plan for St. Peter's in
Vatican City, 1546,
by Michelangelo
is an example of the
centralized Renaissance plan.

The rationale and logic for this change had already been put in place by Heins and La Farge of New York in their 1907 design. A *Seattle Times* newspaper article of December 10, 1905, makes the tantalizing suggestion that the original intent of these architects was indeed to place the altar at the center: *"Under the great center dome will stand the altar."* This did not happen. However, they did leave us with a rather unique legacy in which the cathedral's Renaissance plan is symmetrical around the crossing of the nave and the transepts, with the east and west naves of equal length.

This juxtaposition of the *square*, a human invention depicting material space on its periphery, with the *circle*, a metaphor for the divine without beginning or end, focuses upon a timeless center: *the altar!*

The Altar in the Center

The 1994 renovation and renewal began with an awareness that older church interiors were typically ill-suited to the reformed rites of Vatican II, which call for a change in the focus of liturgical action, to the gathered assembly. Once the architectural aspects and Renaissance layout of the building were recognized, it became obvious to everyone that the altar had to be placed in the center. It was a solution which would encourage full participation in the liturgy while giving harmony to the building's historic features. After establishing this central theme, all the following design decisions flowed from it:

- *Adding the* oculus Dei *(eye of God) in the center of the crossing ceiling directly above the central altar. This returned natural light, missing in the space since the original dome collapsed in 1916.*

- *Removing the two pairs of faux columns and frieze at the face of each transept, thereby restoring an open expanse to the center of the space.*

- *Building a circular altar platform. Though it is of a contemporary design, the platform's Palladian style respects history. The top step has the same diameter as the* oculus *directly above.*

- *Locating major liturgical focal points:* cathedra *(bishop's chair), ambo, presider's chair and cantor's podium at each of the four piers at the crossing.*

- *Designing the four chandeliers located above the altar platform in a different design and layout from those in the naves.*

- *The Blessed Sacrament, according to ancient tradition, is now located in its own chapel. A new* oculus *in*

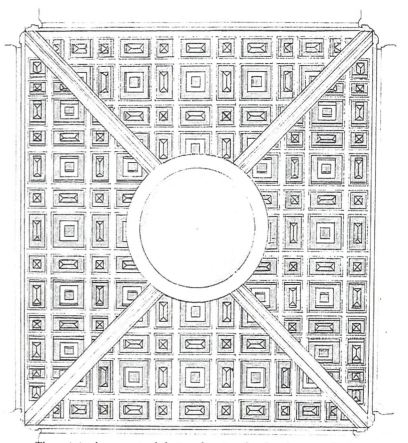

The original conceptual design drawing for the plaster coffering at the crossing ceiling, around the centrally placed oculus.

the chapel's ceiling allows natural light to enter, making a connection between the reservation of the Eucharist here and the actual celebration of the Eucharist at the altar in the cathedral's center. Opposite, on the north side, the Shrine of the Blessed Virgin Mary, a dark space illuminated by votive candles, evokes feelings of both intimacy and infinity.

- *Removing the two transept altars so as not to distract attention from the central altar.*

- *Dropping the old sanctuary floor to the same level as the main space and continuing the diamond-patterned aisle into the east nave.*

- *Heightening the entrance doors around the crossing in accordance with their original design.*

- *Using the quatrefoil motif for the baptistry reflecting the overall shape of the building. This motif can also be found in the Connick stained glass windows dating from 1917.*

- *Removing floor carpeting to reveal the original marble and terazzo floor and improve the natural acoustics.*

In addition to the changes which were inspired by the goals of liturgical renewal, other work included making the building more safe and hospitable with seismic upgrading and new electrical, mechanical, and lighting and sound systems.

To improve the cathedral's poor acoustics for music and the spoken word, and to bring the cathedral's vaulted ceiling into unity with the rest of the classical architectural features, thousands of painted acoustical tiles were removed and replaced with detailed plaster coffers throughout the space.

The coffers were fabricated off-site and were then built into the ceiling. The design and layout are unique to St. James, but reminiscent of the coffering done in great cathedrals and basilicas of Europe, including St. Peter's in Rome.

Skilled plasterers renewed long-lost skills of ornate mold work. They created new cornice details and capitals for the tall columns at each of the four major piers surrounding the central altar. Today, not even a trained eye can discern their work from that done almost a century ago.

View of the scaffolding platform built along the north wall of the east nave so that artisans could construct and paint the ceiling, frieze and column capitals.

Top left: *Off-site, casting plaster is poured into latex molds and reinforced with hemp.*

Top right: *These pieces are then joined together on the ceiling and attached to a metal framework to create the plaster coffering.*

Lower right: *Completed plaster work receives the first coat of paint.*

Lower left: *Dutch-metal gilding is applied by hand, in fact with the painter's fingers, to highlight the plaster detailing.*

Top: *Workers painting the ceiling.*

Center and bottom: *Plasterers constructing ceiling.*

Above: *Close view of the new rosette and plaster coffers against the arch with a row of original rosettes.*

Right: *Design drawing of the coffered ceiling at the crossing.*

Center: *A plasterer reconstructs the capitals at the cathedral crossing with salvaged plaster detailing taken from the cathedral's original frieze, which spanned the transepts.*

St. James Cathedral succeeds in merging contemporary Roman Catholic theology with the original intent of Renaissance architectural design. The hierarchy of ratio, proportion and mathematical clarity gives the space a timeless elegance and results in a clear understanding of the building. The architecture provides a paradox of being welcoming, while pointing to the transcendent.

The cathedral demonstrates that major liturgical changes and functional improvements to a landmark building can be accomplished while still preserving historic integrity. But these are not simply architectural accomplishments. The centralized plan speaks to a church renewing itself by gathering its people around the altar table.

Light pours through the restored ceiling of St. James Cathedral.

We shape our spaces and they, in turn, shape us. What you see and experience today at St. James Cathedral is a sacred space which reveals its inevitable self. That revelation will, over time, impact not only the worshiping community but society itself. ❏

*"And the church must be forever building,
and always decaying, and always being restored."*
Choruses From The Rock
-T.S. Eliot

*Stephen Lee, R.I.B.A. (Royal Institute of British Architects)
is an associate with Bumgardner, a Seattle architectural firm.
He was project architect for the 1994 renovation,
for the installation of the Bronze Doors and
the Archbishop Thomas J. Murphy Millennium Organ.*

a place of RENEWAL

Much to cast down, much to build,
   much to restore;
Let the work not delay,
   time and the arm not waste;
Let the clay be dug from the pit,
   let the saw cut the stone,
Let the fire not be quenched in the forge.

Choruses From 'The Rock'
-T. S. Eliot

A welder works near where the Blessed Sacrament Chapel will eventually be located.

The 1994 renovation began on April 8, the day after Easter Sunday. The project was scheduled for completion just before Christmas with opening ceremonies on December 21 and 22.

Within those eight months, hundreds of workers, including carpenters, steel workers, plasterers, painters and stone masons, descended on the cathedral to restore and renew.

The cathedral's interior during the first weeks of renovation. Work in progress in the far east apse area eventually lowered the level of the sanctuary floor where the altar was previously placed. The scaffolding in the foreground supports a temporary deck for ceiling work above.

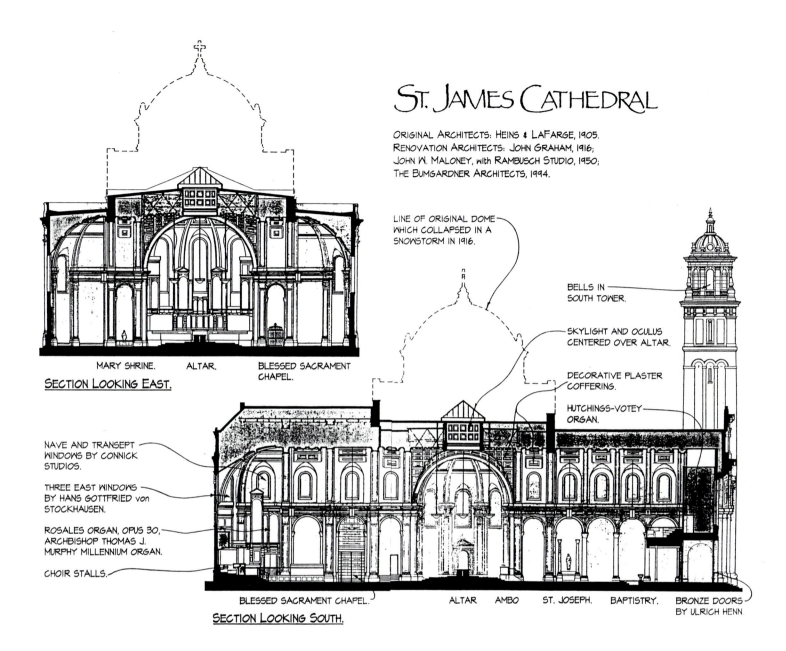

St. James Cathedral

ORIGINAL ARCHITECTS: HEINS & LaFARGE, 1905.
RENOVATION ARCHITECTS: JOHN GRAHAM, 1916;
JOHN W. MALONEY, with RAMBUSCH STUDIO, 1950;
THE BUMGARDNER ARCHITECTS, 1994.

LINE OF ORIGINAL DOME WHICH COLLAPSED IN A SNOWSTORM IN 1916.

BELLS IN SOUTH TOWER.

SKYLIGHT AND OCULUS CENTERED OVER ALTAR.

DECORATIVE PLASTER COFFERING.

HUTCHINGS-VOTEY ORGAN.

MARY SHRINE.   ALTAR.   BLESSED SACRAMENT CHAPEL.

SECTION LOOKING EAST.

NAVE AND TRANSEPT WINDOWS BY CONNICK STUDIOS.

THREE EAST WINDOWS BY HANS GOTTFRIED von STOCKHAUSEN.

ROSALES ORGAN, OPUS 30, ARCHBISHOP THOMAS J. MURPHY MILLENNIUM ORGAN.

CHOIR STALLS.

BLESSED SACRAMENT CHAPEL.   ALTAR   AMBO   ST. JOSEPH.   BAPTISTRY.   BRONZE DOORS BY ULRICH HENN.

SECTION LOOKING SOUTH.

The liturgical principle used in designing the reconfiguration of the cathedral's floor plan was *the assembly as primary minister*. The placement of the altar in the center of the space accentuates the significant role of the gathered community around the table and the symbol of Christ in the midst of the people.

The placement of the Baptistry at the cathedral's main entrance speaks of a journey begun and continued through the nave to the table of the Lord's supper under the eye of God.

The location of the ambo, central and facing the altar as well as the gathered community, focuses on the Word proclaimed, not necessarily on those who proclaim. The same can be said for the placement of the presider's chair and the *cathedra*.

The locations of the Blessed Sacrament Chapel and the Shrine of the Blessed Virgin Mary, separate from the main body of the cathedral and on the north and south sides, give focus to the importance of these sacred spaces and the liturgical actions and rituals which take place there.

the Central Altar

Standing on slate and granite in the light of the dome and in the center of the assembly, the altar is the sign of Christ in the midst of his people. Its central placement speaks of Jesus' abiding presence in the heart of a community of believers, nourishing his people at the table of the Eucharist.

St. James' centrally placed altar, created in the 1994 renovation, was the work of five sculptors. The original panels, now facing west, were created by an unknown Italian artist and taken from the cathedral's old high altar. Three contemporary artists were then asked to interpret these same traditional eucharistic symbols of wheat and grapes for the three remaining sides of the altar table.

The panels on the north side were designed and sculpted by Alaskan Inuit sculptor Larry Ahvakana; those on the south by Northwest artist Mary Jo Anderson; and those on the east were designed by Long Island carver Randall Rosenthall and sculpted in marble by Harold Vogel.

*Top: Archbishop Alexander J. Brunett presiding on Palm Sunday. **Left:** The altar's four sides, beginning top left and going clockwise: the panels facing north, facing south, facing east and facing west.*

Left: Artist Randall Rosenthal's design drawing for the panels on the altar's east side. Top right: After Archbishop Thomas J. Murphy signed the document of the relics, Father Michael G. Ryan, pastor, added his signature. This event was witnessed by the cathedral staff on November 11, 1994. Second right: During a small service, the relics are placed beneath the altar as Archbishop Murphy, Father Ryan and the cathedral staff watch. Third right: The stone masons, and various other workers, lift the marble altar into place, enclosing the relics. Lower corner: The altar's south panels are installed by stone masons. Below: The marble altar panels are unpacked and awaiting installation. Bottom center: Stone masons make final adjustments to the altar's marble surface.

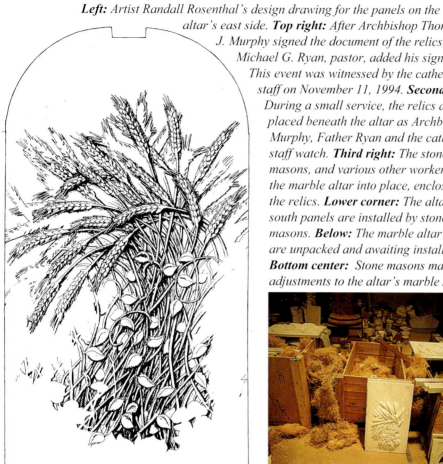

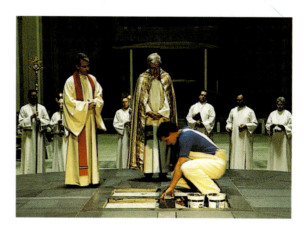

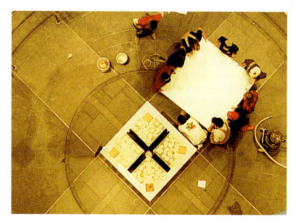

According to ancient custom, beneath St. James' altar lie the relics of saints. On the day of the cathedral's original dedication in 1907, relics of St. Adeodatus, St. Boniface and St. Fortunata were sealed into the cathedral's high altar by Bishop Edward O'Dea.

During the 1994 renovation, they were placed beneath the central altar by Archbishop Thomas J. Murphy, who added the relics of St. Frances X. Cabrini. Mother Cabrini, founder of an orphanage, hospital and school in Seattle, was the first American citizen to be canonized by the Church. She worshipped at St. James in its early years and became a citizen of the United States in Seattle.

the Baptistry

'But you are a chosen race, a royal priesthood, a holy nation, God's own people, that you may declare the wonderful deeds of God who called you out of darkness
into marvelous light.' *1 Peter 2:9*

Above: Section of the flooring around the baptistry. ***Inset:*** *Ukrainian sculptor Vasily Feborouk engraves the inscription in the surrounding floor.* ***Far left:*** *The cathedral's original baptismal font, shown here in the stone workshop during the 1994 renovation, was incorporated into the design of the new baptismal pool.* ***Left:*** *Excavation for the baptismal pool and surrounding floor amid materials assembled for the renovation.*

The wooden forms for the baptistry are secured in preparation for pouring the concrete walls.

Before the pews are installed, workers polish the terrazzo floor surrounding the baptistry.

View from the vestibule of the baptistry at the cathedral's main entrance.

God the Father of our Lord Jesus Christ has freed you from sin, given you a new birth by water and the Holy Spirit, and welcomed you into his holy people. He now anoints you with the chrism of salvation. As Christ was anointed Priest, Prophet, and King, so may you live always as members of his body, sharing everlasting life. *Amen. -Rite of Baptism*

The placement of the baptistry, just inside the main doors of the cathedral's west entrance, demonstrates the role of the Sacrament of Baptism as the gateway to the Church. This is a reminder to all who enter of their first encounter with God through the saving waters of rebirth. Made of marble and slate and in the form of the classic quatrefoil, the baptismal pool reflects the shape of the cathedral itself, with rounded apses to the north, east and south. The engraved inscription surrounding the baptistry, seen on the opposite page, was taken from a baptismal instruction in the New Testament Letter of Peter which declares that all those who are baptized become priestly people, called out of darkness into marvelous light.

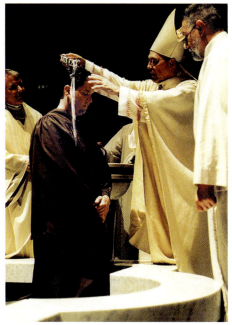

Archbishop Alexander J. Brunett baptizes one of the elect at the Easter Vigil.

__Right:__ The view from the west gallery during a Baptism. Godparents reach out with a pledge to sustain the baptized in faith. Towels, laid to the right of the baptistry, provide a path for the walk from the pool to the vestibule. Two children, at the top of the frame, await their turns while the sacristan wipes water from the previous Baptism. The baptized are then brought to the altar in the midst of the assembly to be anointed. During the Mass they join the community at the eucharistic banquet.

the BLESSED SACRAMENT CHAPEL

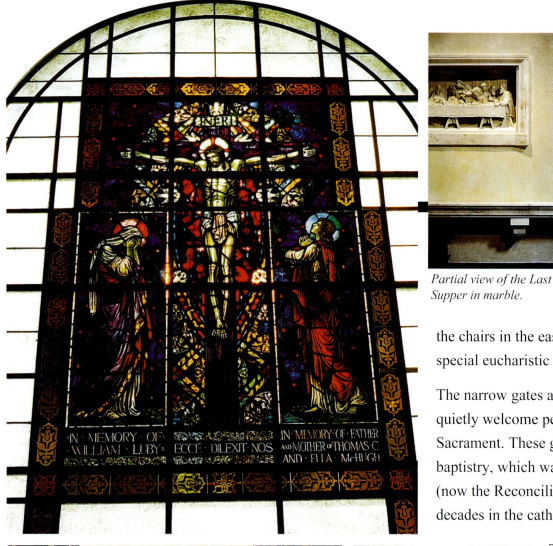

Partial view of the Last Supper in marble.

In accordance with ancient tradition, the tabernacle is located in a chapel separate from the main body of the church in a special place of prayer and veneration. At St. James, the Blessed Sacrament Chapel is located east of the altar and is flooded with daylight from a small *oculus* overhead.

The chapel has two openings. The wide double gates at its north entrance can be swung open and the chairs in the east nave rearranged to face inward for special eucharistic celebrations (shown in lower corner).

The narrow gates at the chapel's west entrance (below), quietly welcome people for prayer before the reserved Sacrament. These gates are from the cathedral's original baptistry, which was located at the base of the north tower (now the Reconciliation Chapel). They gathered dust for decades in the cathedral's basement.

The tabernacle inside the chapel, dating from 1950, is set on the ornate capital of one of four columns removed from the transept areas during the 1994 renovation.

Upper left: *The triptych of the Crucifixion above the north entrance to the chapel.*
Lower corner: *Morning prayer at the north entrance to the chapel.*
Left: *The narrow gates at the chapel's west entrance invite quiet prayer.*

A stone relief of the Last Supper was carved in Carrara marble in Italy for the cathedral shortly after it opened in 1907. It was originally part of the cathedral's old high altar.

The red onyx wainscoting around the base of the chapel's walls is from the 1950 reredos. The floor mosaic, VENITE ADOREMUS, at the west entrance to the chapel, is a near-replica of an inscription found in the cathedral sanctuary area during the 1994 renovation. It had been nearly destroyed in 1950, then hidden beneath carpeting.

The Crucifixion scene in stained-glass above the north entrance (Christ on the cross with Mary and the Apostle John) is Connick glass fashioned into this triptych by the Mayer Stained Glass Studios of Munich, Germany. The three glass panels were originally the centerpieces of the three east apse windows.

The skylight, or *oculus Dei*, in the ceiling of the small chapel was added in 1994 to give a luminous quality to this place of private prayer and veneration.

Above: *The Blessed Sacrament Chapel is accessible from two directions. The double gates at the chapel's north entrance can be swung open and the chairs in the nave rearranged to face the chapel for large gatherings of veneration (as shown on the opposite page during morning prayer).*

Left: *The floor mosaic,* VENITE ADOREMUS, *at the west entrance to the chapel, is shown in progress during the 1994 restoration.*

the AMBO

The *ambo* (or pulpit) is the place where God's holy Word is proclaimed in the midst of the assembly. Like the altar, it too is a source of nourishment for the faithful.

The cathedral *ambo* stands on a stone platform flanked by steps on both sides. The carving on its face was inspired by a passage from Isaiah.

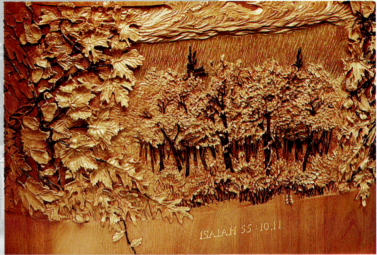

ISAIAH 55:10.11

Sculptor Randall Rosenthal carved the face of the ambo *interpreting the passage from Isaiah in the unmistakable Northwest imagery of clouds, rain and abundant vegetation.*

During the renovation workers move the ambo *into place.*

For just as from the heavens the rain and snow come down and do not return there till they have watered the earth, making it fertile and fruitful, giving seed to those who sow and bread to those who eat, so shall my word be that goes forth from my mouth; it shall not return to me void, but shall do my will, achieving the end for which I sent it.

Isaiah: 55:10-11

Clockwise beginning below: Close-up view of the sunlit oculus *against a dark interior.* **Center:** *A plasterer prepares the base of the* oculus *for gilding.* **Right:** *Architect David Wright paints the inscription at the base of the* oculus. **Right lower:** *Ribbons hanging from the* oculus Dei *over the central altar at Christmas.* **Lower center:** *Architect's drawing of the skylight's design as it relates to the coffering at the central crossing.* **Bottom left:** *Construction workers build the skylight over the* oculus *on the roof of St. James.*

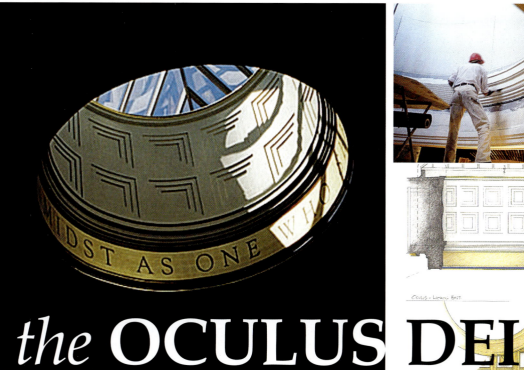

the OCULUS DEI

The *oculus Dei* meets the sky high above the altar in the center of the cruciform structure where the cathedral's original great dome admitted light into its center. The altar is placed directly beneath the dome under the eye of God, as it is in St. Peter's Basilica in Rome.

In February, 1916, the great dome collapsed during a heavy snowfall and was shattered. Finally, since the 1994 restoration, in the place where the dome once stood, a central skylight or *oculus Dei* now admits natural light into the center of the cathedral once again.

The inscription at the base of the *oculus*, which was hand-inscribed, was taken from the Last Supper account in the twenty-second chapter of St. Luke's gospel. It reads, *"I am in your midst as one who serves."*

the Shrine of the Blessed

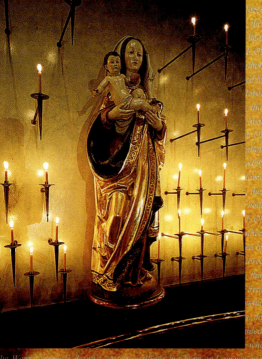

A forest of gleaming candles lures the visitor into the Shrine of the Blessed Virgin Mary. The earthen blackness of the stone floor and the vast darkness above intensify her radiance in the midst of one hundred and seventy small flames.

Mary presides at the head, as if perched on a promontory, with the Christ Child in her arms reaching out to the world.

Virgin Mary

The Shrine of the Blessed Virgin Mary was designed for St. James Cathedral in 1994 by architect Susan Jones, AIA.

the CATHEDRAL CHAPEL

When the Cathedral Chapel was first built it was named Sacred Heart Chapel. Later, when it was used during the winter months for daily Mass in order to reduce heating costs, it became known as the Winter Chapel.

After extensive damage by fire in 1992, reconstruction returned the chapel closer to what was originally intended by the architects. The stained glass window to the east had been hidden within a wall since the 1950 renovation.

The statue of Mary, usually in the chapel's southeast corner, is popularly called "Our Lady of Seattle," because it was brought from Europe to Seattle's first Catholic church, Our Lady of Good Help, in 1870.

The altar is the work of a local skilled woodworker. It was modeled after a fine old credence table which was part of the cathedral's original furnishings. The crucifix above it, used during the Christmas, Epiphany and Easter seasons was fashioned by a local artist from shards of the sacristy's stained-glass windows, which were destroyed during the fire of 1992.

The Madonna and Child with Saints, *by Neri de Bicci, was painted in the early years of the Italian Renaissance (ca. 1471) and now rests on a shelf of white marble taken from the chapel's original altar.*

the CATHEDRAL CRYPT

Archbishop Thomas Murphy lay in state above the cathedral crypt for forty-eight hours while thousands of mourners filed by to pray and pay their respects. Students from the area's Catholic high schools stood guard all the while.

HERE, AWAITING THE BLESSED RESURRECTION,
LIE THE MORTAL REMAINS OF **THOMAS J. MURPHY**
ARCHBISHOP OF SEATTLE FROM 1991 UNTIL 1997.
HE WAS BORN IN CHICAGO ON OCTOBER 3, 1932,
BAPTIZED IN THE PARISH CHURCH OF ST. MEL ON OCTOBER 23,
AND ORDAINED A PRIEST ON APRIL 12, 1958.
APPOINTED BISHOP OF GREAT FALLS, MONTANA,
ON JULY 5, 1978, HE CAME TO SEATTLE
AS COADJUTOR ARCHBISHOP ON MAY 26, 1987
AND SUCCEEDED TO THIS SEE ON AUGUST 21, 1991.
HE SERVED THE CHURCH FAITHFULLY AND DIED
IN THE PEACE OF JESUS CHRIST ON JUNE 26, 1997.
IN CHRISTO GAUDIUM ET SPES

Architect's drawing of crypt and marble flooring.

The practice of interring bishops in their cathedrals is an ancient tradition. In the early Church, Christians wanted to be buried as close as possible to the altar where the Eucharist was celebrated. That led to cemeteries in churchyards.

Canon law states that only bishops may be buried in cathedral crypts, and only saints may be buried below the altar.

The Most Reverend Thomas J. Murphy, the third archbishop of the Archdiocese of Seattle, was the first bishop to be interred in St. James Cathedral's crypt.

He was lovingly lowered to his resting place, just east of the altar, by his pallbearers who included six priests he had ordained during his years as archbishop.

We thank Thee for the lights that we have kindled,
The light of altar and of sanctuary;
Small lights of those who meditate at midnight
And lights directed through the coloured panes of windows
And light reflected from the polished stone,
The gilded carven wood, the coloured fresco...
...We see the light but see not whence it comes.
O Light Invisible, we glorify Thee!

Choruses From 'The Rock,'
T. S. Eliot

The *Labor* of Faith

by Robert Clark

I first came to St. James Cathedral as a convert, and, in the manner of converts, undeliberately and even accidentally. I was not native to the parish or even to the city. Rather, it was where I happened to be standing when, so to speak, lightning struck. I don't mean to say it was a dramatic conversion, but more an experience that, after meandering for years, I stumbled across. When I stood up, dusted myself off, and looked around, there was St. James.

Perhaps the archetypal convert is not St. Paul, thrown from his horse and transfigured on the road to Damascus, but St. Augustine. At the time of his birth in 354, Christianity had been legally tolerated in the then disintegrating Roman Empire for a mere forty years and contended for adherents in a sort of New Age bazaar of pagan and gnostic sects and cults. Augustine's mother, Monica, was herself a Christian and prayed that her son might also become one. But Augustine, sophisticated, cosmopolitan, and gifted with a knack for philosophy and rhetoric, was drawn elsewhere. He took up with the Manicheans, who saw creation divided in a great bipolar conflict between good and evil. Later, he studied neo-Platonism, which held that the dualism that really mattered was not between good and evil but between being and non-being. By the time he was thirty and a professor of rhetoric in Milan, he had come under the influence of Ambrose, Milan's bishop and a compelling homilist and teacher.

His chief desire

Ambrose brought Augustine—now the veteran of most of the pleasures the Roman empire could afford in its decadent phase (as well as the father of a son by one of his several mistresses)—to the verge of conversion, if only the verge. Among all his many writings, Augustine is perhaps best known for the plea, recorded in the *Confessions,* "Lord, make me good, but not just yet." The work from which the words come is less an account of his conversion as such than the multiplicity of ways he for so long evaded or perhaps eluded converting, even once it had become what he chiefly desired in his life. When belief at last came, after every sort of agony and relapse imaginable, it came simply, slyly, like something small, forgotten and unremarkable he had found lying at his feet. He was sitting in the garden of a friend's house. Children were playing next door and he could hear their voices, ebbing and rising in volume and pitch, over the garden wall. Then one of them, with perfect and terrible clarity, said, "Pick it up," as though to him alone. "Pick it up."

At the moment of his conversion, what Augustine picked up was a book, a text of St. Paul. The words his eyes fell upon said, "Clothe yourself with the Lord Jesus Christ, and make no provision for the flesh, to gratify its desires." Thereafter, Augustine was a Christian. It was not that he read these words and resolved to follow them—that he now achieved something he had heretofore failed at—or that he even submitted to something he had been resisting. Rather, his conversion simply befell him. It seemed to Augustine that it was no more or less than a gift, neither earned nor achieved; that even his ability to say "yes" to it was beyond any ordinary kind of willing.

My own conversion seems no more deliberate. I had for years entertained a curiosity about the church, but a mixture of distraction and disdain for organized religion kept me from doing anything about it. Then, in 1995, my wife Caroline and I had a baby boy, and it somehow seemed—regardless of my own doubt and vacillation—that he ought to baptized. St. James was at that time much in the news, having just finished its stunning renovation. And so without much more acquaintance with the parish than that, I went to St. James and asked what would be involved in having Andrew, er, baptized there. Was I a Catholic? Well, no, I admitted and neither was Caroline, although I finally blurted out that I was "curious" about becoming one. We just thought we'd let Andrew go first. I was gently informed that this was not the way it was generally done: That once a baby was baptized into the Catholic faith, the church thought it was a good idea for the child to have some adult—at least one parent and a godparent—to guide him or her in the faith.

Oh, yes, I allowed as that made a certain amount of sense. It was suggested that perhaps I would like to attend the cathedral's Rite of Christian Initiation for Adults (RCIA) classes, test my own interest in the Catholic faith, and then the matter of Andrew's baptism could be returned to. Thus thwarted and not a little stymied, I found myself attending the first of many Wednesday sessions in the Cathedral Hall. The initial sessions were called "inquiries" and were conducted almost entirely in question and answer format. The RCIA process is a Vatican II-ordained program that replaces the somewhat cursory "instruction" adult converts received in private meetings with a priest prior to baptism or, if already baptized in another denomination, First Communion. It is meant to be more systematic, and goes to some length to ensure that conversion is neither hasty nor poorly thought out. In my case, for example, the process lasted almost a year and a half, and at times, contrary to fears of friends who were convinced I was being aggressively recruited into a cult, I felt the church was really trying to discourage me from joining at all.

The people who attended the inquiry sessions ranged from theologically sophisticated intellectuals to immigrants who scarcely spoke English, and the questions ran the gamut from the arcane to the obvious. Just as noticeable were the long silences between questions, as people struggled awkwardly to formulate their queries, to shape, at least in my case, amorphous urges, intimations, and inklings into words. Over the weeks there were dozens and dozens of questions put and answered, but there is one I remember particularly well. An Asian woman whose mastery of English was slight to say the least, timidly raised her arm elbow-high and stammered out, "Why do you people worship statues?"

No one laughed or acted amused. This is, I think, the question about Catholicism that everyone really wants to know the answer to, rather as they once wanted to know how exactly the astronauts went to the bathroom in space. I do not remember who answered—it was either Marianne Coté, a refreshingly down-to-earth lay teacher, or the radiantly serene nun who ran the RCIA program, Sister Frances Wink—or exactly what they said. In any case someone explained that Catholics did not worship images, but honored (or reverenced, if you like) them as signs of the holy, as evidences of God and his saints. Images also function as aids to contemplation and to teaching, but above all as signs, as visible aspects of unseen things. Nor is a sign the same thing as a symbol: A graphic representation of flames is a symbol of fire, but smoke is a sign of it—something that is of the fire, but not the fire itself.

An attraction to faith

This view of the way God's presence is visible in the world—the manner in which "God is in all things, and profoundly, intimately so" as St. Thomas put it—is one of the fundamentals of Catholic teaching and is called sacramentality; and it is among the main attractions of the faith for me. So it was that an apparently naive and foolish question posed by an uneducated woman who could barely speak my language got to the nub of everything I was trying to give voice to. I later came up with the analogy that in the sacramental view we see God as we see light under a doorway. We do not directly see the source of light, the flame, but the sign of the light, not a symbol or words describing the light but its emanation, and that is as a fact to us.

The church's seven official sacraments are formally ordained rites which enact such signs. But properly seen, the world is abrim with sacraments, with signs, not only as phenomena and things but as persons. And I cannot but think that the woman who posed that question was, for me at least, a sign herself. That moment, that sign was, in retrospect, for me a little like St. Augustine's voice in the garden. And at St. James I would encounter more of them.

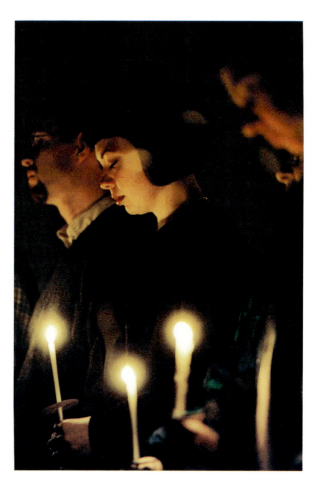

At Easter Vigil

I at last became a Catholic in 1997, at Easter. Along with fifty other converts, I took my First Communion and was confirmed at St. James Cathedral during the Easter Vigil Mass, late on the Saturday night before Easter Sunday. This is how, we are told, it was done in the earliest days of the church. We stood in the dark, listening to readings from Genesis through to the resurrection, and gradually, almost imperceptibly more and more candles were lit.

Then we stood before Father Michael Ryan, pastor of the cathedral, and Archbishop Thomas Murphy. Archbishop Murphy was dying of cancer and would be buried in this place only two and a half months later.

Normally, the archbishop would perform our Confirmations, speaking words of committal to us and signing our foreheads with oil. But we had been told that this would be done instead by Father Ryan. The Archbishop was so weak and the risk to him of infection in touching us all so grave, that he would merely preside. But that was not how it was. Instead, the Archbishop stood, beaming, and set his hand on each of our fifty heads. I was tired as I waited my turn, I had been in this church late at night for two hours already. I was not bored or unhappy or irritated, but neither was I going to have an epiphany or transfiguration here. I was only moved, turned a little from where I had been, quietly converted here and in a hundred inconsequential instances, re-bound to what I had always been.

Archbishop Thomas J. Murphy in St. James Cathedral in May, 1997 about a month before his death

I reached the front of the line and Father Ryan told the Archbishop my name. Then he raised his hand to my head and said the words. He was pallid and weathered in the way of the near-dead, but he smiled and I felt the pressure of his hand on my head. It was a hand reaching out of and through death to bring me into this new life. Love, aching and weary, was stronger than death after all.

Andrew was baptized by Father Ryan in the full daylight of a Sunday morning a week later. Caroline and I stood on one side of the font, and his aunt, uncle, and maternal grandmother stood on the other. I held him, although at eighteen months, he was too big to be held on his back as baptized infants are. He looked busily around and when the water was poured on his head, he cried out with irritation, in a tone of affronted protest that made the congregation laugh. Then we moved down the aisle to the altar where Andrew was to be anointed with oil, just as I had been in my Confirmation. I was tense as I waited for Father Ryan to come around to us. Andrew's first outburst was more amusing than embarrassing, but, as his struggling in my arms seemed to indicate, he was now about to go into full toddler-meltdown.

But when Father Ryan reached us, Andrew merely looked at him quizzically. Then he signed Andrew's head with oil and said, *"He now anoints you with the chrism of salvation. As Christ was anointed Priest, Prophet, and King, so may you live always as members of his body, sharing everlasting life,"* and Andrew continued placidly to regard him. We returned to our seats, where Andrew busied himself with the little pencils and pledge cards and such that are in the pew.

Archbishop Alexander J. Brunett baptizes an adult at Easter Vigil, 1998.

I would like to say that his sudden silence was more than a burst of composure, that it was an uncanny but real sign of his assent to the rite he was participating in. But that is too tidy and facile. The assent was mine, his mother's, and his godparents', given on his behalf, which, if he wants, he may reaffirm at his own Confirmation. For now, however, he is oblivious to it, and that is as it should be. Unlike his ancestors and their successors down to me, he is not troubled by whether he believes or if his belief is real and true. His life takes its measure not from fact but on faith. He is two years old. He knows nothing. He believes everything.

It is not that way with me. Scarcely four weeks after Easter, my doubt was at times a nagging itch. I do not doubt the things the church teaches and which I affirmed at Easter. They seem plausible enough, mysteries though they are. Rather, I doubt my assent to them, my continuing ability to hold them as I feel I ought to, to believe them aright. The church understands this. Its founder, the first pope, Saint Peter, was the epitome of doubt. Jesus had to scold him for having only "little faith," and after the resurrection questioned him three times about his love. That is why "religion" is "binding again"; that is why "conversion" is "turning"; they are not only movements but repetitive movements. Conversion and the practice of religion are the taking on of a perpetual labor as perennial and quotidian as housework. Faith is never complete, at rest in the same state, or located in the same place because we are ourselves in motion. We are forever needing to turn and be turned toward it; to discover and be discovered by it.

As a Catholic, the locus and center of my faith is the Eucharist, the Mass. To my former Protestant sensibility, the most outrageous teaching Catholicism propounds is the real presence of Christ in the consecrated bread and wine at Communion: That these elements are not merely symbols of Him in a commemoration of something He did two millennia ago, but are Him, become Him in a sacrifice identical with the Last Supper itself. In the Catholic sacramental world of signs, the Mass is the *ne plus ultra*. So if I do not believe in that, the core of my faith is at stake. And, having been a Catholic for hardly a month, I was not sure, halfway through the Mass, that I did.

We had said the *Sanctus*, the great prayer that inaugurates the consecration, and at its end the congregation knelt for the consecration itself. As Father Ryan began to pray over the elements, a feeling of dread began to overtake me, a fear that by the time the elements became God, I still would doubt that they were God. I was in a sort of race with my disbelief, my lack of conviction as the Eucharistic prayer drew towards its climax. I felt harried and distracted as well, and that sense was not being ameliorated by the children in the pew behind me. They were talking—probably not loudly to anyone's ears but mine—and moving, apparently drawing or coloring in order to occupy themselves through the Mass. I couldn't get a look at them, because they stayed mostly on the floor, hidden behind the wall of the pew-back.

But that was neither here nor there. The children continued to draw and to talk, but the moment was upon me. Father Ryan raised the bread and then the wine—"This is my body." "This is my blood"—and the bells signifying the Consecration rang, and the wafer hung in the air before me like a bone-white moon; and what, what, if anything did I believe?

I did not know. I had stopped breathing in the last few seconds and now I felt a little stunned, as though I seen something very sudden and appalling and was still taking it in. And I began to think again and to wonder if I had any faith; or if, after all these years—through all my enthusiasms and agnosticisms—I had any business here at all.

The congregation had begun to rise, and I began to lift myself from my knees, scarcely aware of the people around me, sealed in the vacuum of my dread and fear. Then I heard a voice behind me, over the wall of the pew, but clear and bright as the tone of a tuning fork shimmering at my ear. It said, "This is for you," and after a pause it said it again, as if I might not have been listening. "This is for you."

I stopped breathing again, and then let my breath go and turned around. One of the children behind me had risen from the floor and was handing her mother the drawing she had evidently just completed. Her mother thanked her and remarked how pretty it was.

I knew it was only a coincidence, but I took this as a sign, as anything might be a sign, rightly seen, since *Deus est in omnibus rebus, et intime* (God is in all things, and intimately). You can make as much of it or as little as you like: Only its being—its givenness occurring alongside one's own givenness—is of consequence. But I took it as sustenance, as Augustine took up the book and read. For almost two years, I had pursued altering the religious commitments not just of my own lifetime but of twenty generations of Clarks, and throughout that journey I wondered whether I was right or had any right to do it. And a child's voice heard over a wall told me that, Of course, I did. And that has been enough, most of the time, to keep me coming back to the Mass; to go on putting my unbelief before the presence of God, my dogged faithlessness—my belief in nothing rather than something—before His Being. Sometimes I see what a small thing becoming bread and wine in the Eucharist must be for Him—a mere substantial sleight of hand—and what a great and, to us, unimaginable thing, is His becoming us; taking on our life, right down to our disbelief in Him, taking it on—love so great it will nullify its own being in order that we may be.

That incident was but one sign among many. More dramatic and uncanny than most, perhaps, but scarcely isolated. St. James is for me less a place than a landscape of signs, a highway whose guideposts steer us along the unceasing journey that is the labor of faith. It seems to me apt, for example, that when we enter the cathedral, the first thing we encounter is the baptismal font; we begin—each time, again—where we first began our lives as Christians. Then we make our passage down the nave (the word itself comes from the Latin for ship) to the altar, less a destination than the hub of a wheel along whose spokes and around whose perimeter we travel, a home to which we return as members in a community of faith.

At one time, the Blessed Sacrament was reserved here on the altar, but as part of the renovations it was installed its own chapel to one side of the altar. That move caused some controversy, because some people felt that the Real Presence, what was most central to the faith, was being moved from the center of the Cathedral to its periphery. But I think there is another way to interpret this in the field of signs that is St. James. In fact, this location seems to me appropriate, for we never approach the great mysteries of our faith directly—they wouldn't be mysteries if they could be so apprehended—but only obliquely, at, as it were, an angle, "through a glass darkly." And so at St. James we come to the Blessed Sacrament—which is nothing less than the mystery of the Incarnation itself—from the side rather than head on, passing from and through the altar which is the locus of our collective prayer as the church, as the people of God we become through Baptism.

There is one more sign I want to mention, to which all the other signs in a sense point. What I discovered in

overhearing that child offer her drawing to her mother was two things: That "this," the church and its sacraments and signs, is indeed "for" me, but also that this gift that comes of the labor of faith is reciprocal; that I am "for" the church, and in particular the community that is St. James. So the labor of faith does not end in my own prayers, devotions, or participation in the liturgy any more than the signs of the cathedral itself end at the altar. Rather, the one labor entails another labor whose sign is, we might say, literally above and beyond the altar. For in the dome of the Cathedral, at its very apex and center, are written the words, *"I am in your midst as one who serves."*

As with the Blessed Sacrament, it is a truth we approach from the side and, in this case, from below as well. But it is the same truth: The fact of the Incarnation as it manifests itself among us and, through service, in us. And this sign—for I find at St. James every sign points to another sign—leads back to that first sign I encountered at St. James back in RCIA, that of persons; hundreds of persons who in dozens of tasks incarnate the church as the people of God both inside and outside the cathedral. Like the signs contained in the fabric of the building, some are readily apparent to anyone who attends Mass, for example, the ushers, lectors, Eucharistic ministers, altar servers, choristers and musicians. Behind the scenes—behind these more public signs—are the persons who serve in tending the building and the grounds, replenishing the candles and flowers, answering the telephone and stuffing envelopes, staffing the bookstore, writing, editing, and producing publications, and brewing coffee and offering hospitality.

Beyond these are the ministries that serve to bring persons into the church—through Baptism, religious education, Confirmation, and RCIA—as well as the ministries that bring the church to persons often not only outside the traditional boundaries of religion but at the margins of society: the poor, the sick, the hungry, the displaced, and the homeless who are served through programs like the Family Kitchen, Nightwatch, AIDS Support, and ESL. In their midst, among the forgotten and hopeless and destitute—the least loved of us whom our faith asks us most to love, in whom we are commanded to see the face of Christ —sign meets sign, does by food or shelter or mere companionship its saving work and brings itself home now twice-graced to St. James to share itself again.

Beside these living signs and their sacramental action, it might seem that the cathedral, the building itself, is beside the point; that the physical, created world is of a lesser order than these manifestations of spirit and of our ideals. But as a writer, I have to subscribe to William Carlos Williams's precept, "No ideas but in things." We come necessarily to know the real only through the concrete. We come to things through other things: our knowing is analogous and imaginative rather than direct; one thing connects to another, and then, slowly or of a sudden, we come to see a little of how it really is. It is that way with art, and even more so with the great mysteries of faith. We approach them by and through signs.

It seems to me now that the daily labor of faith is inevitably tied to the labor of service, and that the one sustains the other. The doubt I struggled with on that Sunday shortly after my reception was answered by a sign at St. James, the product of a child laboring to make something beautiful for her mother. In doing so, she made something beautiful and sustaining for me, although she will never know it. That is how it is with signs; we cannot know how or when or in whom they will come. But I have come to believe that St. James Cathedral will always have them in abundance if I have eyes to see them.

I think perhaps my favorite place in the cathedral is the chapel of the Blessed Virgin. It, too, is off to one side of things, and for me its gifts come from seeing how one sign becomes another, and how all those things call us into faith and into service. I love the image of Our Lady that stands at the head of the chapel, but I think I like the ceiling best of all, a blue-black dome with the images of stars set on it that suggest that there is no ceiling there at all. It could be night with nothing above me but space and light from the stars, or perhaps they are becoming something else. I think

of the words of the poet Giovanni Cerri: *"Fireflies are daughters to the stars/and go in the countryside to catch the scent of hay/which is the scent of God/because it smells of work."* ❏

Robert Clark has been a St. James parishioner for four years and is the author of five books of both fiction and non-fiction, most recently, My Grandfather's House: A Genealogy of Doubt and Faith.

a place of MERCY

God has shown the
    strength of his arm;
God has scattered the proud in
    their conceit.
God has cast down the mighty
    from their thrones,
    and has lifted up the lowly;
God has filled the hungry
    with good things,
    and the rich
God has sent away empty.
    'The Magnificat'
    Luke 1:51-53

St. James Cathedral has been a beacon of light high on a hill for nearly a century calling out a welcome to those in need. Inspired by Christ's example of mercy, the people of the many ministries of St. James light the darkest nights with compassion, easing the burdens and bringing dignity to the lives of the poor and vulnerable.

"Truly I tell you, as often as you do it for the least of my brothers and sisters, you do it for me."

Matthew 25:40

Jesus with two disciples at Emmaus.

Jesus with two disciples at Emmaus
North window, top

"I was hungry and you gave me food...I was hungry and you did not give me food."

Whatever we offer each other, whether it be a smile, a piece of bread, tender love or a helping hand, Jesus will take all that as done to Him: "You did it to me."

Jesus meets the women of Jerusalem.

Jesus meets the women of Jerusalem
North window, bottom

"I was a stranger and you welcomed me...I was a stranger and you did not welcome me."

To offer a home to the homeless Christ, we must start by making our own homes places where peace, happiness and love abound, through our love for each member of our family and for all our neighbors. Once we have learned to love with a love that hurts, our eyes will open and we will be able to give that love.

The windows high in the east apse are the work of both the Connick Studios of Boston and the Mayer Studios of Munich, Germany. Each of the outer two windows has three depictions of Christ, painted by the celebrated stained glass artist, Hans Gottfried von Stockhausen. His drawings, shown below, represent Jesus' parable about the Last Judgment in images of his own Passion, Death and Resurrection. At St. James, these windows inspire those who serve in his name to discover his face in the faces of those who suffer. The commentaries in the text accompanying each of the sketches of the roundels were written by Mother Teresa of Calcutta.

Jesus thirsts
South window, center

"I was thirsty and you gave me something to drink...I was thirsty and you did not give me something to drink."

"I thirst," said Jesus on the cross. He spoke of his thirst not for water, but for love. He, the Creator of the universe, asked for the love of His creatures. He thirsts for our love. These words, "I thirst," do they echo in our souls?

Jesus thirsts.

Jesus is taken captive
South window, bottom

"I was in prison and you visited me...I was in prison and you did not visit me."

One day, we will go to meet Christ in heaven. Our Lord will show His gratitude and He will say, "Come! Come to me, you blessed of my Father, because I was hungry, you gave me to eat; I was naked, you clothed me; I was homeless, you took me in."

Jesus is taken captive.

One day, we will go to meet Christ in heaven. Our Lord will show his gratitude and he will say...

The Catholic Worker Family Kitchen

Christ took the side of the poor and powerless and his example challenges us to see the world through the eyes of those most in need. A commitment to 'community' and to Christ's message of compassion are the motivation behind St. James Cathedral's *Catholic Worker Family Kitchen*.

The Family Kitchen serves dinner every day to an average of 150 low-income residents and homeless individuals in the area. The goal is to serve nourishing food and to create a warm inviting place where people can feel safe, relax and make friends.

Daily, volunteers line up at the windows offering great pans of hot food and greeting the guests who move forward slowly in quiet concentration, negotiating trays and dishes with canes and tote bags. St. James' Family Kitchen embodies the example of Jesus: the last are first and take their seats at the table while the able-bodied serve, wait and clean up.

"Make me worthy, Lord, to serve my neighbors throughout the world who live and die in poverty and hunger. Through my hands, give them this day their daily bread; and by my understanding love, give peace and joy. Amen."

Mother Teresa

"Come! Come to me, you blessed of my Father, because I was hungry, you gave me to eat; I was naked, you clothed me; I was homeless and you took me in."

The St. James Winter Shelter

Gingham tablecloths are taken up and sleeping mats are laid in the gaps between the tables as another St. James social outreach ministry takes over Cathedral Hall. Winter Shelter provides a place for fifteen homeless men to sleep for the night.

This homeless shelter is a preferred refuge for men who live on the streets. By comparison, it offers more space between mats than other shelters and a healthy hot breakfast in the morning.

The St. James Winter Shelter is operated by parishioners during the winter months when the city's other shelters are full. Because a small, yet welcoming volunteer staff is on duty throughout the night, fifteen men are not sent back to the streets.

English as a Second Language Program (ESL)

The St. James ESL Program teaches English to low-income refugees and immigrants so that they may lead fuller lives in a new country.

The program serves over 120 individuals every year with one-on-one tutoring and classes in conversational techniques, providing special services to youth and the elderly. St. James' ESL is nationally recognized as a model program.

Amidst a CLOUD of WITNESSES

by David Buerge

The autumn chill did not dampen the devotion of those gathered to witness the long-anticipated event. A little before 3:00 p.m., His Excellency, Edward O'Dea, Bishop of Seattle, accompanied by Bishop John Carroll of Helena, Montana, and Bishop Augustine Dentenwill of New Westminister, British Columbia, left the little wooden St. Edward's chapel at the corner of Terry and Columbia in Seattle and strode down the street to the great hole in the ground where a maze of brickwork and scaffolding hinted at future grandeur. Wielding his gilded crosier and followed by virtually every priest in the diocese, O'Dea led the trio, resplendent in brilliant vestments and crowned with golden miters, between long lines of representatives from many Catholic orders and societies across the country, all eager to witness the ceremony blessing the cornerstone of the greatest cathedral in the Pacific Northwest.

As they approached the stone on its temporary altar to sprinkle it with holy water, the choir began the Litany of the Saints. The air, sweet with incense, pulsed with rich Gregorian chant as the procession offered prayers next at a small wooden cross marking the future site of the main altar and then returned to the hollow stone where O'Dea deposited coins, inscriptions in glass bottles, and medals and mortared the lid shut with a silver trowel. Finally, all joined in the stirring hymn, "Holy God, We Praise Thy Name."

It was November 12, 1905. Washington was only fourteen years a state, and the ceremony, which marked so important a moment for the Catholic community, looked to the past as well as the future. The dioceses of the three attending bishops recalled a time when their territories belonged to the huge ecclesiastical province of Oregon City, established by Pope Gregory XVI in 1846, the first Archdiocese west of the Mississippi and only the second in the United States. When land north of the Columbia River became part of the new diocese of Nesqually, erected in 1850, its first bishop, Augustine Magloire Blanchet, made the little wooden St. James mission church, built several years earlier by the Hudson's Bay Company next to Fort Vancouver, his cathedral. Enlarged in 1856, this historic first cathedral, looking rather sweet with its narrow, crowned steeple, was replaced in 1884 by a larger, more impressive brick structure built nearby in Gothic style and dedicated in honor of St. James by Blanchet's successor, Bishop Aegidius Junger.

The cathedral's building committee was comprised of the day's Catholic civic and business leaders. Bishop O'Dea, center, 1906

The second St. James was a source of pride for Washington's Catholics, who vied with Portland across the river in a race to see who would be first to complete the construction of their cathedral. Yet the land the church stood on was involved in a bitter legal dispute lasting nearly fifty years, revealing how vulnerable the church was to the pervasive anti-Catholicism of the times. At one point, federal troops occupied the brick cathedral; the arson that reduced the little wooden church to ashes was never punished, and the rancor born out of these humiliations lasted generations. The grandeur of the third St. James in Seattle, begun by O'Dea, was in part a gesture of defiance from a growing community that often felt marginalized.

A cathedral is more than a building. According to canon law it is the bishop's church, specifically the site of the chair, *cathedra* in Latin, from which he presides. The man who invited Bishop O'Dea to move his see to Seattle was Father Francis Xavier Prefontaine, the bluff, civic-minded priest who grew up with the city and built his church, Our Lady of Good Help, down by the lava beds, the rough land reclaimed from the tide flats, where the workers and tradesmen and their families who made up his flock lived. He came in 1867 when the raucous logging town had only 600 people and his first congregation consisted of two ladies.

At first, Blanchet refused him permission to purchase property, arguing that Seattle was a lost cause. But by 1890, with more than 40,000 people, the emergent city was ready to surpass Portland in size and dominate the Pacific Northwest and Alaska.

The cathedral's high altar after 1926, when the organ, seen in the background, was installed

Left: The Right Reverend A.M.A. Blanchet, consecrated Bishop of Walla Walla September 27 , 1846; transferred to Nesqually, May 31, 1850; resigned 1879, died February 25, 1887.
Far left: The Right Reverend Aegidius Junger, D.D., consecrated Bishop October 28, 1879, and served until death in December, 1895.
Lower left: The Most Reverend Edward John O'Dea, D.D., J.C.D., consecrated Bishop of Nesqually September 8, 1896; see transferred to Seattle September 11, 1907, died December 25, 1932.

In August 1896, shortly after learning that O'Dea had been named third bishop of Nesqually after the death of Junger, Prefontaine organized a committee of six prominent laymen to invite his Lordship to establish his episcopal residence in their city. In a letter listing its advantages, the call to arms rings clear. "Because of Seattle's predominant influence in the political, social and economic affairs of the state," they warned, "she has become and will remain the headquarters and chief battleground of all the elements hostile to the church. The morale of the church militant requires the inspiring presence of her leader where the battle wages fiercest."

O'Dea recognized the advantages and the threat as clearly as Prefontaine, and he cultivated his own contacts with prospective benefactors, among them the Irish-American silver kings of Spokane who hoped the bishop would relocate in their city. O'Dea weighed his options carefully and in 1902 purchased a city block on Seattle's First Hill, far above Prefontaine's church, surrounded then by saloons and bordellos. In 1904 he hired the prestigious New York firm of Heins and La Farge to design an immense

structure "in 14th century Italian Renaissance style with twin towers soaring 175 feet into the sky," that would blow away the competition. If its $225,000 price tag caught the breath, the huge walls rising from the earth thrilled the eye.

The spectacular building was opened to the public on December 15, 1907, for a recital given by a celebrated organist. Dr. Franklin S. Palmer, the cathedral's music director, performed on a great pipe organ donated by the Baillargeon family, that filled the western end of the nave. Those crossing the terrazzo floor of the vestibule read the words set in mosaic tile calling to mind the purpose and the hope of the great church, DOMUS DEI PORTA COELI: "House of God, Gate of Heaven." Originally, Heins and La Farge planned that the main altar should be located at the building's most dramatic point directly beneath the great dome, where transept met nave. But instead it was placed at the eastern end and drama was provided by a grandiloquent baldachino that rose above it like an exclamation point. Assisted by three bishops, O'Dea dedicated the cathedral with great pomp on December 22, sealing the remains of three saints, Adeodatus, Boniface and Fortunata, into the altar during the Solemn Pontifical High Mass, and reading from the pulpit, (an extravagant work of marble and ormulu), the Papal Bull changing the diocese from Nesqually to Seattle.

The cathedral dominated the city. Inside, lay people and religious organizations contributed many of its sumptuous furnishings. Mrs. Elizabeth Foss provided the main altar and baldachino. The graceful statues of the Sacred Heart, the Virgin and St. Joseph, all carved from white Carrara marble, were the gifts of individual donors.

So were the altar of the Sacred Heart, carved from Washington marble, and the pulpit, baptistry and the stations of the cross. The rich velvet carpet had been donated by the ladies of the cathedral parish and the maple altar rail by the Knights of Columbus.

Saint Frances Xavier Cabrini

A Saint in Seattle

When Frances Xavier Cabrini slipped in to worship at St. James Cathedral, she was an energetic missionary, establishing schools, orphanages and Columbus Hospital, a near neighbor to the cathedral.

She was enthusiastic about Seattle in 1915, continuing work begun when she had first arrived in 1903: "Now I am negotiating the purchase of a house [the Perry Hotel] for a school or an orphanage. The city has a population of 200,000 and is built on hills. We are about to place ourselves on a strategic hill which dominates the bay and the city. The bishop is so good that he helps and gives us support. Our Italians are happy and proud to have an Italian organization; their houses are located in the valley at the foot of our hill." It was, of course, First Hill.

At first Bishop Edward O'Dea encouraged her to buy the furnished property at

The fact that so many had a hand in making this the grandest church in the Northwest made O'Dea's silver jubilee of ordination, celebrated four months after the dedication, even more of a triumph. In June the first priestly ordination in the cathedral dramatized the community's growth, and in September Father Prefontaine was honored for his decades of work with the robes of a monsignor. But the old man was nearing his end. Five months later he died, and on March 9, 1909, the community gathered for the first of one of the most moving of all services held in the cathedral, the singing of the Requiem Mass as it bids a servant goodbye. Pride tempered sentiment on that occasion as the eulogy recalling humble pioneer beginnings resonated in the gleaming vault rising where, only decades earlier, silent forest had ruled.

But pride and great buildings often prove a dangerous mix. Poor design and construction methods affected the truss work holding the dome and lantern above the intersecting nave and transept. Almost 400 tons of masonry rested on four steel girders designed to hold only 180 tons safely. When nearly two feet of wet snow added its weight during a winter storm in 1916, the result was catastrophic.

The day was February 2, Candlemas day. Snow had begun to fall early, and after morning Masses a deep white blanket kept visitors away. World War I was at its height; a bloody stalemate in France dominated the news, and some of the candlelight flickering in the cathedral's majestic stillness that afternoon doubtless commemorated distant trouble. At quarter past three, unable to bear their burden any longer, the girders buckled and gave way, sending the dome tumbling 80 feet to the floor with a boom loud as a cannon shot. The air of compression hurled heavy oaken pews against the walls and blew out windows.

Running from the residence, the pastor, Father William M. Noonan, and his priests stared aghast at the mountain of rubble filling the church and the snow drifting down through the ragged hole gaping above them. Noticing William O'Connell, recently appointed editor of the *Catholic Northwest Progress*, nearby, Noonan could only raise his finger in admonition. "Now Willum," he cautioned in his brogue, "not a word of this to the press!"

The cathedral's roof after the collapse of the dome, February 2, 1916

Only eight years had passed since its dedication, and the cathedral appeared a ruin. Fortunately, repair proved possible, and O'Dea carried out a major restoration lasting a year. Those who attended the reopening on March 18, 1917, noticed a dramatic change in the building's layout. A flat timber roof covered the hole where the dome had been, and the ceiling at one end was fifteen feet lower. Instead of a large, cruciform space, the interior had been reconfigured into a processional corridor by the architectural firm of John Graham and Associates. To the line of columns marching forward from the back were added four massive piers and colonnades in the transepts, all directing the eye toward the sanctuary where the baldachino was replaced with a new high altar backed by an elaborate reredos. The acoustics were better. While the dome had been in place, the only one who could be heard clearly during Mass was Bishop O'Dea himself.

Although much decorative work had been destroyed, O'Dea's expenditures and the generosity of the patrons ensured that, if the interior was somewhat reduced in scale, it was certainly more elaborate. The pulpit and communion rail, crushed beneath the rubble, were replaced by the original donors, and the new high altar, carved from Italian marble, included a deeply cut relief of the Last

This view toward the south transept shows the rubble from the collapsed dome that filled the interior of St. James.

Madison Street and Boren Avenue for its modest asking price, $200,000, money she did not have. Opposition to the project closed doors to her throughout the city. She wrote the needed sum on a slip of paper and placed it on a book in the hand of a statue of St. Ann. Her prayer for $190,000 was soon answered, largely through Mr. Hilberg, a Swedish Jew of the Scandanavian Bank of Seattle, who offered her a loan. The neighborhood was up in arms.

"They gave vent to their fury," she wrote, "by passing around a petition to the effect saying they did not want a children's home in this beautiful section of Seattle." Contributors canceled pledges, and "Would you believe it? Even the bishop's lawyer and the cathedral priests began to work so that we would not acquire the property."

Withdrawal of financial support made it necessary to prepare the Perry Hotel as a self-sustaining facility, a plan suggested by the bishop. The Missionary Sisters reserved as many beds as possible for indigent patients but were compelled to charge fees in the new sanatorium and maternity home which was to become Columbus Hospital. Mother Cabrini later called it "my difficult work in Seattle."

Difficult beginnings evoked commitment and reliance on God, the ingredients of real success, she believed. The ministries of her Missionary Sisters reached an ever-expanding population. Columbus Hospital was later renamed in her honor, serving Seattle until 1991. St. Paul's Foundling Home cared for children till the 1950's. Sacred Heart Orphanage has evolved into Villa Academy School, which continues to educate young minds and hearts.

History had also been made in Seattle. Here Francesca Xaveria Cabrini, born in 1850 in Lombardy, Italy, became a naturalized citizen of the United States

Christ's resurrection, depicted in stained-glass, was installed high above the south transept. The cathedral's windows, commissioned in 1916, are the work of the Connick Studios of Boston which provided windows for 5,000 religious and civic buildings worldwide from 1913 to 1986.

Supper in its base. On the ceiling where the dome had been, an artist reproduced a vivid fresco of Raphael's *The Ascension*. By 1919, donors had replaced the cathedral's plain glass windows with a glorious series of stained glass panels. Designed by the Connick Studios of Boston, representations of the ten commandments, the nativity, the resurrection, the four evangelists, Saint James and Saint Patrick illuminated the interior.

There was talk of building a larger, grander dome—the piers had been built for that—but the $150,000 cost of repairs added to an already huge debt made such plans impossible. O'Dea had levied a $100,000 assessment upon all the parishes of the diocese to help defray costs, but the cathedral parish remained hobbled by debt. In winter Masses were said in the smaller, adjoining Sacred Heart Chapel to reduce heating costs. If money was tight, gifted individuals employed skill and devotion to enrich the liturgy. Under the guidance of Dr. Palmer, the men and boy's choir gained national acclaim, and non-Catholics as well as regular parishioners crowded services to hear them. Once again, the Baillargeon family stepped forward and installed another pipe organ behind the main altar, a companion to the first, that could be played in tandem with it or alone. Elaborate wooden screens flanking the reredos and choir risers enhanced the beauty of the sanctuary.

Dr. Palmer's Schola Cantorum
*helped the cathedral
gain national acclaim.*

Clergy and laity had labored mightily to make the cathedral a source of inspiration, but it was only one of a suite of associated buildings. A rectory was built in 1909, followed three years later by a four-story brick building housing the St. James Cathedral School, with the lunchroom as the parish hall. To accommodate demands for more classroom space, work began on a boys' high school east of Terry Avenue, and on March 16, 1924, the bishop dedicated the new facility named O'Dea High School in his honor. Diagonally from the cathedral stood Columbus Hospital, built by Mother Cabrini, canonized in 1946 as the first American saint. East was Seattle College (now Seattle University) and further north on Capitol Hill, Seattle Preparatory School, both built and run by the Jesuits. Nearby were Holy Names Academy, Forest Ridge and Immaculate High School for Girls. These institutions and the large number of substantial Catholic homes surrounding them gave this part of Seattle the name 'Catholic Hill.' In only a few decades Catholics had made their presence felt.

O'Dea celebrated the golden jubilee of his ordination in the cathedral on Thanksgiving Day, 1932. It was his last public appearance. During his episcopate, the northwestern church witnessed amazing growth: the diocese became two when the Diocese of Spokane was erected in 1913; the number of Catholics had grown from 40,000 to 324,000 and their churches statewide, from 89 to 262. He died on Christmas Day, and his Requiem Mass in the cathedral he built marked the end of a vigorous era.

in 1909. She was canonized in 1946, the first American citizen proclaimed officially a "Saint" of the Catholic Church.

Francesca had first dreamed of China. The burning love of Christ inspired her to found the Missionary Sisters of the Sacred Heart, presumably China-bound. But Pope Leo XIII turned her eyes "Not to the East, but to the West!" where Italian immigrants were languishing without spiritual guidance or human resources.

Mother Cabrini first crossed the Atlantic in 1889. In New York and throughout North, Central, and South America, she lived by the motto, "I can do all things in Him who strengthens me" (Phil. 4:13). Crisscrossing the ocean, she brought Italian women into the mission fields of urban America.

Everywhere she and her sisters made God's love tangible by their own faith and kindness.

Impressive as her hemispheric accomplishments were, they do not make a saint. And it was a saint who prayed in St. James Cathedral, a saint whose relics now lie beneath its altar and before whose statue in the west nave dévotées still light candles. Letters leave clues to her holiness and to the energy that drove her:

"She who has virtue possesses peace, and no one can take it from her. Do you understand? She can give peace even to those who refuse it."

"In each orphan we see a case worthy of compassion."

Mother Cabrini's relics lie beneath St. James Cathedral's altar. Her many institutions still benefit thousands, but her greatest legacy is the light of a love which brightened so many lives, a beacon reflecting the face of God.

-Sister Mary Cabrini Durkin O.S.U.

The Sisters of the Holy Names of Jesus and Mary taught the students in Catholic schools in the area and in the cathedral school throughout the decades. Here, three Holy Names sisters stand outside the Frye mansion, later replaced by the cathedral convent. A relic of the founder of their religious Congregation, Blessed Mother Marie Rose Durocher, is venerated in the sacristy of St. James Cathedral.

If O'Dea had been a builder, the man who took his place, Bishop Gerald Shaughnessy, S.M., saved his work from bankruptcy. With a background in finance, Shaughnessy had been appointed to do just that, since by the time of his consecration in September, 1933, the Great Depression was at its height and Seattle was hard hit. The diocese was broke and nuns were literally dying in their convents from malnutrition. His strict, even draconian methods often dismayed those who came pleading for help, and his prickly personality won him

few friends, but many admired the battles he waged with bankers for debt relief. While keeping an eye on the bottom line, Shaughnessy did not neglect his pastoral duties. From his cathedral chair, sermons and letters expressing his support for labor and concern for the poor earned him national attention.

An outdoor Palm Sunday procession led by acolytes, Bishop Thomas Gill and Archbishop Thomas A. Connolly, passing before the cathedral, 1950's.

The Most Reverend Gerald Shaughnessy, S.M., S.T.D., appointed Bishop of Seattle on July 1, 1933, died May 18, 1950.

While he and the cathedral pastors struggled to pay down the debt, the parish itself grew poorer. The rich gradually moved to affluent suburbs, and the hotels and apartments replacing many of their fine homes housed a burgeoning wartime population. The absence of fathers in the armed forces and of mothers working in defense plants, however, put many young people at risk. To help address this problem the pastor, Monsignor John Gallagher, organized Ca-Teeners, a program to help parish teenagers whom he drafted by the score to serve at the altar. At Sunday High Mass, as many as fifty boys dressed in magenta cassocks and white surplices carried candles, sang in the choir or assisted at the liturgy. Despite an uphill battle, the parish paid off its debt by 1945.

Bishop Shaughnessy was the only prelate on the West Coast to publicly protest mistreatment of Japanese Americans during World War II, and he assigned several priests to serve those interned in relocation camps. Through his efforts the entire diocese emerged from its financial struggle on a sound financial footing, but his labors took their toll. Late in 1945 he suffered a stroke, followed by others that left him incapacitated. He was unable to work but refused to yield responsibility. A curtain of silence descended around him. When it became obvious to insiders that there was no hope of recovery, Bishop Thomas A. Connolly, auxiliary to the Archbishop of San Francisco, was appointed coadjutor bishop.

Left: The original cathedral chapel, The Chapel of the Sacred Heart, was called the Winter Chapel.
Below: The renovated chapel in 1950 came to be called "Our Lady" Chapel. Its centerpiece was the painting The Madonna and Child with Saints, *a masterpiece of the early Italian Renaissance done by Florentine artist Neri di Bicci.*

Connolly cultivated a regal style and when he was elevated to archbishop in 1951, he invited 25 bishops and abbots to attend his elaborate installation at St. James. The reception following drew the largest crowd ever to the Civic Auditorium—people hungry for leadership, whom he did not disappoint. Coming from sunny California, he was struck by the drab condition of the cathedral complex which, except for the chancery that Shaughnessy had rebuilt in 1939, had of necessity been allowed to deteriorate. The cathedral itself had grown dirty and dim. Tattered wallpaper and plaster hung from the rotted ceiling and bricks could be pulled from the walls with little effort. Clearly, it needed repair.

Connolly began by directing local architect Paul Thiry to redesign and add a third floor and convent wing to the rectory. Then, to help fund the cathedral's renovation, he inaugurated a drive during the diocese's centennial anniversary, raising more than a million dollars. He hired the New York design firm of Harold Rambusch and local architect Ralph Lund to restore the edifice, an effort that ultimately cost $500,000–twice the original building cost—and the results were impressive.

Archbishop Thomas A. Connolly presides at a solemn High Mass in the 1950's.

Steam cleaning removed nearly forty years of grime, revealing the original golden hue of the exterior brickwork. New copper sheathed the tower cupolas, and a carillon was installed so that the cathedral bells could be rung electronically. On the west facade, a huge black and gold glass window portrayed the Lord framed by grape vines and symbols of the northwestern church nurtured by resources of the forest and sea, illustrating the scriptural phrase, *"I am the vine; you are the branches."*

Additionally, statues of St. Frances Cabrini, St. John Vianney and St. James filled its formerly empty niches. Inside, steel beams replaced rotting roof timbers, and the heating, ventilation and wiring systems were modernized. Plywood and plaster rococo ornament transformed the reredos into a showier

The Most Reverend Thomas A. Connolly, D.D., J.C.D., consecrated Auxilary Bishop of San Francisco August 24, 1939; appointed Coadjutor Bishop of Seattle with right of succession on February 28, 1948; succeeded May 18, 1950; retired February 25, 1975; died, April 18, 1991.

backdrop for a dramatic wooden statue of St. James and a pedestal for two gilt angels. The ceiling was covered with echo-absorbing acoustical tiles painted with vivid designs that were illuminated by new chandeliers, and the floor was covered with a rose-colored carpet. Northwestern artist Eustace Ziegler depicted the Baptism of Christ in a six-by-nine-foot oil painting for the north tower baptistry. Also, the chapel of the Sacred Heart, dubbed the Winter Chapel in more frugal times, was entirely redone and rededicated as Our Lady's Chapel, having as its centerpiece the painting *The Madonna and Child with Saints,* a masterpiece of the early Italian Renaissance done by Florentine artist Neri di Bicci.

But before this work could be completed, Bishop Shaughnessy died on May 18, 1950. With St. James under renovation, the funeral had to be held in the Immaculate Conception Church in the city's Central District. As one straightened chapter closed, another opened onto phenomenal growth. Connolly was another builder *par excellence*, and he matched the explosive growth of the region's Catholic population with construction on a monumental scale. What had been considered a lavish outlay for the cathedral's renovation was barely one half of one percent of that spent building up the diocese. And while churches, schools and convents mushroomed, the refurbished St. James hosted ever-grander celebrations for the northwestern church. Thirty-two bishops attended the Mass celebrating the diocese's centennial jubilee. Even more dignitaries assembled

The Most Reverend Raymond G. Hunthausen, consecrated Bishop of Helena on August 30, 1962, appointed Archbishop of Seattle on February 25, 1975, retired August 21, 1991.

for glittering ceremonies elevating Seattle to an archdiocese in 1951, and New York's Cardinal Spellman presided at the golden jubilee Mass for the cathedral parish.

When Archbishop Connolly retired in 1975 and Bishop Raymond G. Hunthausen of Helena, Montana, became Archbishop of Seattle, the church was alive with new hope encouraged by the Second Vatican Council. Hunthausen had been appointed Bishop of Helena in 1962 and did his on-the-job training in the heady and challenging atmosphere of the four sessions of the Second Vatican Council. Imbued with the council's vision that the church was *people* before all else, Hunthausen committed himself to giving the people their baptismal birthright, insisting they share responsibility with him for the life and ministry of the Church.

A humble yet strong leader, Hunthausen had the common touch and inspired many with his transparent goodness and attractive, down-to-earth spirituality. He had the soul of a prophet and used the pulpit of the cathedral to speak out on controversial moral issues of the day. His stand against the nation's nuclear arms buildup soon became legendary, but so also did his outspoken advocacy on behalf of the poor, the homeless, the unborn and the elderly. And while not a "bricks and mortar"

The Most Reverend Thomas J. Murphy, D.D., S.T.D., ordained Bishop of Great Falls on August 21, 1978, appointed Coadjutor Archbishop of Seattle on May 26, 1987; assumed the office of Archbishop on August 21, 1991; died June 26, 1997.

During the cathedral renovation in 1994, Masses were held across the street in the O'Dea High School gymnasium (affectionately dubbed "St. Gym" by parishioners).

bishop, he nonetheless inspired and instigated the 1994 restoration and renovation of the cathedral. He was convinced that the holy people of God would only be strengthened by praying in a building that reflected the great theological vision of the Second Vatican Council.

Hunthausen retired in 1991, several years after a controversial Vatican visitation which threw the archdiocese into turmoil by calling into question some of his pastoral decisions. He was succeeded by his coadjutor, Archbishop Thomas J. Murphy, a Chicago priest who most recently had served as Bishop of Great Falls-Billings, Montana.

Murphy quickly won the hearts of the people with his warm Irish ways and his uncanny ability to be present to just about everyone. He energetically gave his support to the cathedral renovation plan already on the drawing boards, working with the cathedral pastor, Father Michael G. Ryan, to give the grand church the layout originally envisioned for it by Heins and La Farge. They were convinced that this layout,

On the night of the cathedral's dedication, Archbishop Thomas Murphy holds high the architectural blueprints which were presented to him as part of the dedication rites by principal architect Donald Brubeck, A.I.A., December 21, 1994.

with a centrally-placed altar, would take maximum advantage of the cathedral's symmetrical and cruciform floor plan and greatly enhance the active participation of the faithful.

A full year of meetings would take place, however, before the new archbishop and the cathedral pastor could begin raising money to translate dream into reality. And even before that had begun, the cathedral hosted one last celebration to mark its splendid past. Archbishop Connolly died in the spring of 1991 as old as the century, and his funeral was celebrated in the about-to-be renewed St. James.

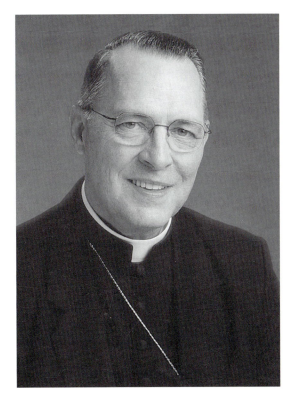

The following year, a million-dollar fire, set by a mentally ill transient, would heighten the need to finish the fund-raising and get the work of renovation underway. The incident, reflective of the neighborhood's continuing transformation as hospitals, clinics and halfway houses replaced homes and residences, did not provoke intolerance for the marginalized among parishioners, but actually rekindled a zeal to serve the poor as they renewed their cathedral. Borrowing from the words of Dorothy Day, the "20th Century apostle to the poor," Father Ryan reminded his parishioners that "for many who are poor, a cathedral is the only beautiful place they can come to every day."

The Most Reverend Alexander J. Brunett, D.D., Ph.D., ordained Bishop of Helena, Montana, July 6, 1994; appointed Archbishop of Seattle October 28, 1997; installed December 18, 1997.

But a beautiful cathedral was not enough. In the parish hall volunteers at the Catholic Worker Family Kitchen continued serving hot meals to the area's low-income residents and, responding to a new need, parishioners began hosting a winter shelter for homeless men in the Cathedral Hall. Characteristically looking to the needs of those in the far reaches of his archdiocese, Archbishop Murphy worked vigorously to raise funds to assist the thousands of unemployed in the suffering timber communities of southwest Washington.

The first fruits of the long-planned renovation was the beautifully restored chapel, reopened on December 7, 1993, with di Bicci's masterpiece, sans soot, glowing on a marble shelf, a fragment of the shattered old altar. Previous to the renovation, it had hung over a stained glass window that had been plastered over in 1950. Once again light poured through the lovely window—an ironic gift of the flames.

Then, on Easter Monday, 1994, the doors to St. James closed and a vanguard of more than 200 artisans and workers assembled to begin in earnest the major work of the renovation project. Between then and December, passersby strained to catch glimpses of the gutted interior, marveled at heaps of rubble dumped outside, and lit hopeful candles before images of saints painted on the gray plywood fence barricading the main entrance. On the 22nd of that month, 87 years to the day after Bishop O'Dea had dedicated it, a dozen bishops, 200 priests and more than 1,000 representatives from parishes throughout the Archdiocese assembled in the new, resplendent St. James to celebrate another milestone in the history of the northwestern church.

"St. James the Magnificent"

"St. James Cathedral was a late-bloomer.
It waited 87 years to come into its own."

Seattle *Post Intelligencer,*
Saturday, Dec. 24, 1994

Eight million dollars were spent, less than the original estimate, more than critics thought prudent; yet who could deny the magnificence it purchased? Bronze bells rang from the towers; a coffered ceiling and the removal of carpets produced brilliant acoustics; and once again those entering through the main doors could read the words announcing the purpose and the hope of all these earthly labors: DOMUS DEI PORTA COELI, "House of God, Gate of Heaven."

Moving into the nave, the space dramatized the soul's journey through the waters of Baptism all the way to the heavenly banquet symbolized by the gleaming altar, now finally at home in the center of the cathedral and brilliantly illumined from above. Beyond, the east apse windows, gloriously completed and unobstructed, quietly told of the baptismal call to love the poor and serve the needy.

The chapter of the cathedral's spectacular renovation closed all too soon, however, when Archbishop Thomas Murphy, a magnetic and immensely popular leader, was called home from his labors. Fittingly, Murphy was laid to rest on July, 3, 1997, in the cathedral's episcopal crypt built but never used by Bishop O'Dea, nor by his successors.

A few months later, the maturing community assembled to welcome his successor, Archbishop Alexander J. Brunett of Helena, Montana, at his installation on December 18, 1997.

Archbishop Brunett's long experience as a pastor and his years of high-profile involvement in the field of ecumenism and interreligious affairs seemed just the right blending of gifts in the leader who would help usher a growing archdiocese into a new century and a new millennium. His strong commitment to the multicultural makeup of the archdiocese, first proclaimed in twenty-six languages at his Mass of installation, soon saw

*Archbishop Alexander J. Brunett
presides at Midnight Mass, Christmas, 1999.*

him welcoming in the cathedral groups as diverse as the Filipino community (Simbangabi), the Vietnamese community (Lunar New Year), and the Spanish-speaking communities (Madre de las Americas). Seizing the moment made even more auspicious by the archdiocese's milestone one hundred-fiftieth anniversary, the new archbishop quickly and wisely made it clear that past glories would not be enough. Like his brilliantly renovated cathedral, the past would be highly honored, but only to light the way toward a future filled with hope.❏

*David M. Buerge has written several books and articles on
Northwestern themes, particularly religious history. He, his wife Mary
Anne and their children are members of St. Catherine's Parish in Seattle
where he teaches at the parish school. Buerge is currently completing a
biography of Chief Seattle.*

a place of Pilgrimage

St. James Cathedral is named for St. James the Greater, the patron saint of pilgrims. Above the north entrance to the cathedral, a statue of St. James shows him carrying a pilgrim's staff. The shell has been his symbol since the Middle Ages. St. James was one of Jesus' closest companions, ascending with him to the Mount of Transfiguration and waiting in the Garden of Gethsemene.

pilgrimage to the **Cathedral**

HOUSE OF GOD, GATE OF HEAVEN

For centuries, Catholics have made pilgrimages to holy places such as Jerusalem, Rome and Spain's Santiago de Compostela, where tradition says St. James is buried. Like the hermits of the ancient desert, pilgrims leave their homes, their worldly possessions and superficial concerns, to journey together to a sacred place to pray.

St. James is a sacred place. Thus, people from throughout the archdiocese and the nation make pilgrimages to St. James Cathedral.

Native Americans, Latin Americans, Asian Americans, Pacific Islanders, African Americans and others from the region's diverse communities make pilgrimages to the cathedral to participate in liturgies which celebrate their cultural heritage.

Christians of every denomination come weekly to the cathedral's Friday evening ecumenical service to pray together in simple, meditative chants patterned on similar services held at the ecumenical monastery in Taizé, France.

Pilgrimages are made not only from outside St. James Cathedral, but from within. Each year parishioners move as a body of pilgrims with palms on Palm Sunday, with the Blessed Sacrament on the Feast of Corpus Christi, and to the cross on Good Friday.

Pilgrimages are inner journeys as well as an external ones, interior assents and descents within the self to find God.

Clockwise, upper left:
Archbishop Alexander
J. Brunett takes a flame
from the outdoor fire
which will light the
Paschal candle and the
candles the congregation
carries during Easter
Vigil.
Left: Paco Lerma comes
to the cathedral in
traditional dress, Madre
de las Americas
celebration.
Below right: Traditional
Filipino Santo Niño
procession
Lower left: A hospital
ministry chaplain
processes with the oil
of the sick during the
Chrism Mass.
Center left: Camolinians
(Pacific Islanders) carry
the Chamorros banner
down St. James' center
aisle at a Marian
celebration.

Top left: *On Palm Sunday people gather for the Palm Sunday procession. At a ceremony in O'Dea High School, Archbishop Brunett blesses the palms. Then members of the cathedral's choirs line the route to the cathedral and greet the pilgrims processing with song. The procession begins with the ministers; then the congregation, singing and walking, processes into the cathedral carrying blessed palms.*

Top right: *Representatives of the Samoan community come to the cathedral for a ceremony honoring their heritage. They are welcomed by The Most Reverend Alexander J. Brunett.*

Center right: *During the Veneration of the Cross on Good Friday, people come forward to show a sign of respect. Here, a man kneels and kisses the cross.*

Bottom right: *Native Americans process down the center aisle of the cathedral during the traditional cedar blessing.*

Bottom left: *Father Michael G. Ryan and Archbishop Alexander J. Brunett walk in the Palm Sunday procession.*

a Holy Place

All Christians are called to holiness. The Church fosters holiness within us through the celebration of the sacraments, through the teachings of Jesus, and through the fellowship of believers.

...holiness through the celebration of the sacraments...

Archbishop Brunett blesses the sacred chrism. The chrism is used throughout the archdiocese for Baptisms, Confirmations, priestly ordinations and dedications of churches and altars. The chrism is reserved in the cathedral's ambry along with the oil of the sick and the oil of catechumens.

the Cathedra

Left: *Architect's draft rendering of the archbishop's* cathedra
Above: *Archbishop Alexander J. Brunett seated at the* cathedra, *the episcopal chair*

The cathedra is the bishop's chair. Taken from the Greek and Latin word meaning 'chair,' the *cathedra* is one of the primary symbols of the cathedral. It is here that the archbishop presides over sacramental celebrations.

With the reemergence of cathedrals as great centers of urban life in the Middle Ages, they became the place where schools were erected and maintained. The chair is symbolic of the bishop's role as teacher and pastor of the local church.

The carved wooden pediment and columns which frame St. James' cathedra are historic pieces taken from two earlier *cathedre* within this space.

...through the teachings of Jesus...

His agenda was to announce Good News, to heal the sick, to free the oppressed, to feed the hungry, and to spend time with sinners. This is the church's ministry, too.

the Central East Apse Window

Baptism embraces the worshiper at St. James Cathedral from the great bronze ceremonial doors, to the baptismal pool, all the way to the east apse, where the central stained-glass window is a catechism of Baptism in sunlight and glass.

At the top of the window, Jesus is depicted standing in the waters of the Jordan. John the Baptist is on one side and an angel on the other. Over Jesus' head and down his body flow the waters of rebirth. Above him, the heavens stand open and the Spirit of God hovers, the same creative Spirit who hovered over the dark and chaotic waters at the dawn of creation.

In this window, the cool waters do not stop at Jesus in the Jordan; they flow downward and become the waters of the Red Sea through which Moses and the chosen people escape to the Promised Land. And the waters transform yet again, flowing ever back through time to become the waters of the great flood over which Noah and his family floated to life.

The Christian walks from the waters as God's beloved, and, like Jesus, begins a life of ministry. His agenda was to announce Good News, to heal the sick, to free the oppressed, to feed the hungry, and to spend time with sinners. This is the Christian's ministry too.

Baptism does not stop at the waters, it begins there. Its promise lives on in acts of faith, compassion and mercy.

nd holiness through the
fellowship of believers.

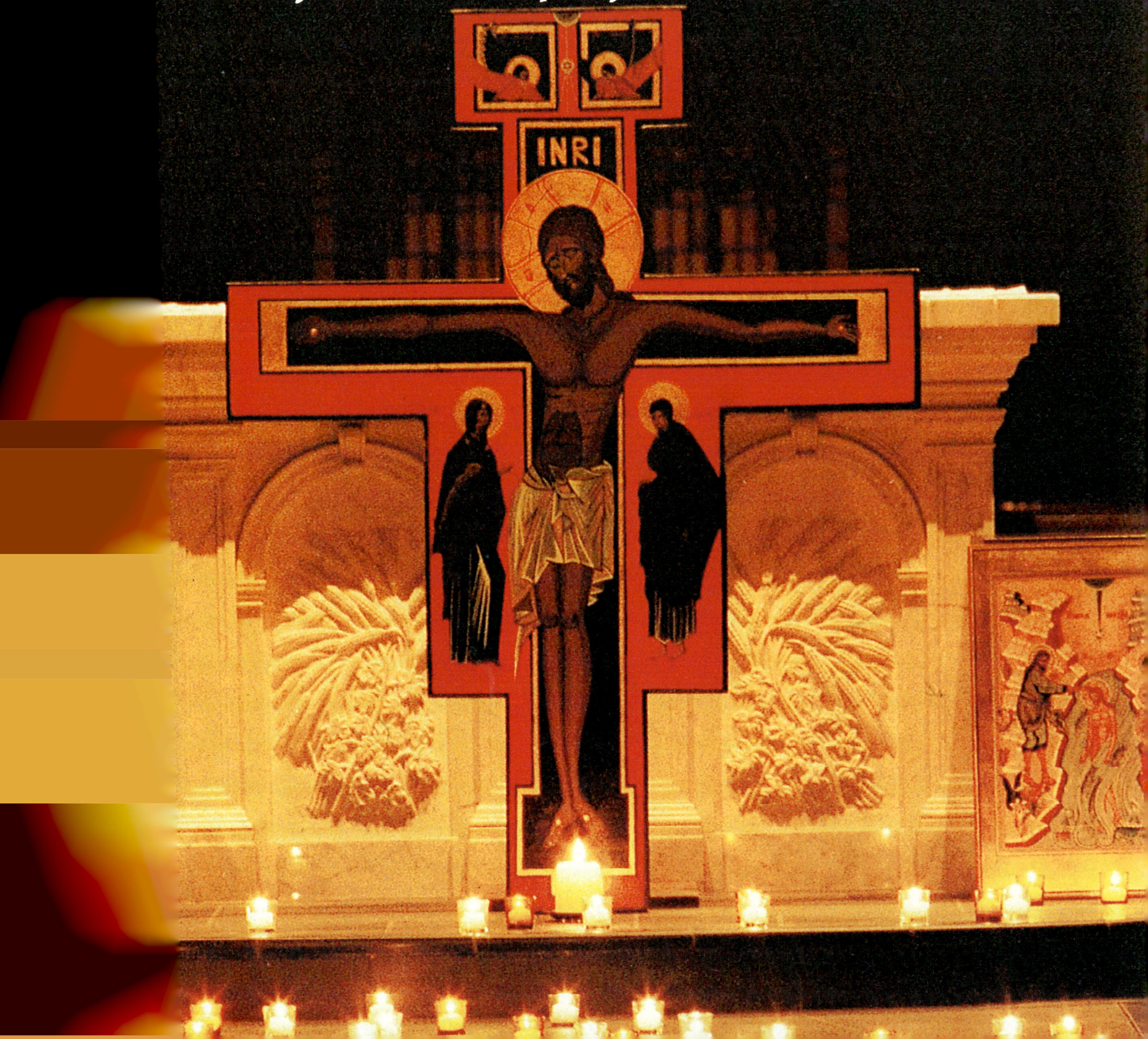

Upper left: *Workers at the St. James Family Kitchen serve their brothers and sisters who come for a meal and a place to make friends.*

Upper right: *Archbishop Alexander Brunett greets members of the Native American community at an ecumenical service at the time of his installation, December, 1997.*

Center left: *Sister Anne Herkenrath, SNJM, and parishioners at the cathedral's annual picnic. The city blocks off the streets on the Feast of St. James every year and parishioners enjoy a picnic under a canopy of trees.*

Center right: *Pals at the cathedral's annual picnic watch the performing clown.*

Bottom: *Sister Claudette Conrad, SNJM, (second from right) and "God's precious cargo." The Cathedral's two Vans make the rounds every Sunday to pick up parishioners who need transportation to church.*

Opposite page: *An icon of Jesus on the cross is displayed at the "Taizé" prayer service every Friday night. This weekly service has been an ongoing part of the cathedral's prayer for a decade and has gained a following among young Christian adults from many area denominations. The prayer is patterned on similar services at the monastery of Taizé in France where monks of the Reformed and Roman Catholic traditions have developed a distinctive style of simple, meditative chants, now popular around the world. The community of Taizé works to foster unity among all Christian denominations, rooting ecumenism in a life of common prayer. The quiet grandeur of St. James Cathedral is an ideal setting for this beautiful, meditative service.*

the Cathedral Icons

I cons are windows into the eternal world. St James has a large collection of festival icons written by cathedral iconographer, Joan Brand-Landkamer who works on cherry wood panels with tempera and 23k gold leaf. Images, such as seen here, of Christ, the Blessed Virgin Mary and saints are carried in liturgical procession and enthroned in the cathedral for prayer and veneration.

Our Lady of Vladimir

The Presentation at the Temple

The Marriage Feast of Cana

The Dormition of the Virgin Mary

Palm Sunday: Journey into Jerusalem

Illustration by Maria Laughlin

St. James the Greater

An overbold desire

The people of the parish of St. James feel a special affinity for our patron, a humble fisherman and preacher who traveled to the ends of the known world.

In the Gospels the name of James is always linked to that of his brother John. Jesus "walked along from there and saw two other brothers, James, the son of Zebedee, and his brother John. They were in a boat, with their father Zebedee, mending their nets. He called them, and immediately they left their boat and their father and followed him." These are extraordinary young men. They follow without hesitation, without asking questions and without looking back.

James and John appear most prominently in the Gospels when their mother quite literally pushes them forward and asks that they be given seats of honor in the heavenly kingdom:

"Then the mother of the sons of Zebedee approached him with her sons and did him homage, wishing to ask him something. He said to her, 'What do you wish?' She answered him, 'Command that these two sons of mine sit, one at your right hand and the other at your left, in your kingdom.'

"Jesus said in reply, 'You do not know what you are asking. Can you drink the cup that I am going to drink?' They said to him, 'We can.' He replied, 'My cup you will indeed drink, but to sit at my right and at my left, this is not mine to give but is for those for whom it has been prepared by my father.'

When the ten heard this, they became indignant at the two brothers." James and John, with bold, thoughtless haste, ask not only to be the closest to Jesus in his kingdom, but also to be a little above and a little apart from the rest of the chosen twelve. The other apostles are deeply annoyed by the effrontery of James and John. Saint John Chrysostom remarked, "See how imperfect they all are: the two who tried to get ahead of the other ten, and the ten who were jealous of the two!"

And yet, there is a great deal of love and faith mingled in James' and John's overbold desire. They love without thinking twice; and this love leads them into extravagances. Clearly a great change has been accomplished in these simple and unambitious fishermen in the course of less than three years. They had once been satisfied with seats in their father's boat; now their hopes know no boundaries; they are going to heaven "by paths untrod."

The death of James is related briefly in the *Acts of the Apostles*: "King Herod laid hands upon some members of the Church to harm them. He had James, the brother of John, killed by the sword." James drank the cup Jesus drank, and was the first of the twelve to be martyred; and thus he gained the precedence he so desired. His martyrdom won him the title by which we distinguish him from the other apostle of the same name: "James the *Greater*."

-Maria Laughlin

The Most Reverend Alexander J. Brunett, Archbishop of Seattle

PROCLAIMING THE WONDERFUL WORKS OF GOD

AFTERWORD
The Most Reverend Alexander J. Brunett

Whenever I gather with the people of our archdiocese in St. James Cathedral, I realize how truly blessed we are. It is not just the striking beauty of the cathedral that prompts this thought. Many cathedrals are strikingly beautiful. No, the real blessing of St. James is its unique power to gather the people of God in a way which celebrates the holiness of God even as it honors the holiness of God's people.

When the Fathers of the Second Vatican Council called for the "full and active participation" of the faithful in the celebration of the liturgy they were making a strong statement about the baptismal dignity of each member of the church, a statement that unleashed a whole chain of consequences affecting everything from the language of worship to the very shape of the buildings in which that worship is celebrated. Church buildings quickly took on a new importance: they were now to help awaken the baptized to a priestly identity and empower them to *"proclaim the wonderful works of God who has called us out of darkness into marvelous light"* (1 Peter 2).

The Archbishop preaches from the cathedral's ambo.

That was a tall order, especially for wonderful old churches like St. James. And too often, in trying to respond to it, church renovators swept away a glorious past to accommodate present demands. Or, conversely, and just as unfortunately, they allowed a timid and nostalgic devotion to the past to compromise the rightful exigencies of the reformed liturgy. The unique achievement of Seattle's St. James Cathedral, in my judgment, is the comfortable and even seamless way it joins past to present and, in the process, points confidently to the future. Even the casual visitor to St. James finds it impossible to be certain what is old and what is new—no small achievement, but an important one because the Roman Catholic liturgy itself lives in three dimensions, making the past present in the joyful hope of future glory.

But there is more: Seattle's Cathedral is just as successful at sending people forth as it is in gathering them in. The community which is shaped and formed so intentionally around the centrally placed altar under the watchful *oculus Dei* is constantly going out from the cathedral with a renewed commitment realizing outside the building the full meaning of what they have done inside. In this way, the Last Supper words of Jesus high above the altar, *"I am in your midst as one who serves,"* become more than words. Those who pray in St. James Cathedral bring them to life in their loving service to the poor and vulnerable.

On that chill November day in 1903 when Bishop Edward J. O'Dea laid the cornerstone for St. James Cathedral, he couldn't possibly have foreseen what his great cathedral would become and how many lives it would touch and transform over the years. From my vantage point a century later, I cannot begin to envision what role the cathedral will play at this beginning of the third Christian millennium, but of this I am certain: St. James Cathedral will, from high on its hilltop, continue its strong and silent watch over a great city even as it shapes and challenges and transforms the people who help make that city great.

House of God, Gate of Heaven

St. James Cathedral's Bronze Ceremonial Doors were opened for the first time to greet the Third Christian Millennium, Christmas, 1999.

From the Editor:
Embracing the genius of St. James Cathedral with this book leaves me in awe and deeply grateful. The Master Builder builds through innumerable devoted faithful. Foremost among them is Father Michael G. Ryan who first inspired me to take on this project, then trusted me, offering expert guidance throughout. There is no doubt that his faith and passion for this House of God have been the catalysts for so many who have applied their gifts to this place.

The work here has not been done cautiously. Cautious is not in the vocabulary because God is not in hiding at St. James Cathedral. You can find God's work in the creative whirlwind of James Savage and in the persistent drive of Larry Brouse diligently and capably attending to the excruciating details. Both contributed to the production of this publication.

A special appreciation must go to Stephen Lee, project architect for the 1994 renovation who devoted so many years to this place. Together we pored over hundreds of photos, our faces glowing from the light of the slide table and the computer screen. He believed we could do it, I was unsure, and by God, we did.

Jackie O'Ryan is director of public affairs for Catholic Community Services of Western Washington and a parishioner at St. James Cathedral.

Acknowledgments

Photographers:

Craig Harrold, who photographed the cathedral's interior throughout the 1994 renovation, is a commercial photographer in Seattle specializing in corporate people and places for local and national clientele. He and his family are parishioners at St. James Cathedral.

Robert De Giulio is a freelance photojournalist and painter living in Seattle with his wife and daughter. His photographs include those accompanying author David Brewster's Heart of the City essay.

Stephen Lee, R.I.B.A. (member Royal Institute of British Architects), is an associate with Bumgardner Architects in Seattle and was project architect for the cathedral's 1994 renovation. Lee provided many photographs and all of the architectural drawings for this publication.

Mike Penny is a Seattle-based commercial photojournalist who has contributed regularly to the Catholic Northwest Progress.

Randall J. Corcoran provided the photograph of The Great Easter Vigil, 1995, on the facing page of the pastor's foreword. He is a Seattle based architechtural photographer and a parishioner at St. James Cathedral.

James F. Housel provided the photos of the Shrine of the Blessed Virgin Mary.

Additional photos provided by: **Sam Miller**, **John Wiley** and **Vilem Sokol**.

Our gratitude to **Michael L. Reichert**, president of Catholic Community Services of Western Washington and the Archdiocesan Housing Authority, whose appreciation for this work made it possible; to the photo archives of The Archdiocese of Seattle, The Catholic Northwest Progress, The Seattle Times, The Seattle Post Intelligencer and The Museum of History and Industry; and to Bumgardner Architects for printing services.

House of God, Gate of Heaven graphic lay-out by **Jackie O'Ryan** and **Antéprint,** France.

Publisher: Editions du Signe - B.P. 94 - 64038 Strasbourg - France
Publishing Director: Christian Riehl
Director of Publication: Dr. Claude-Bernard Costecalde
Publishing Assistant: Sylvie Asimus
Copyright Text: © 2000 St. James Cathedral, Seattle
Copyright Design and Layout: © 2000 St. James Cathedral - ISBN: 2-7468-0049-7

United States Library of Congress registration and copyright information is available upon request.

Printed in Italy by Albagraf, Pomezia